Radiant

By

Brit Kuhn

Radiant

Author's Note:

Trigger Warning! This book has all the triggers, every commandment broken (literally). This story is based on Brit's recollections of the moments in time that has shaped her very being. Brit has tried to seek the light in darkness that was always close by and chooses to live with faith instead of fear.

It should be noted that names and places have been changed throughout this book to protect the privacy of those involved. This story offers so many lessons that can offer healing elsewhere. All shadows should be brought to the light to achieve healing. You can never heal what you refuse to reveal.

As you read Brit's story, reflect on your own healing journey. It takes a very strong individual to sit with themselves, calm their own storms, heal without trying to bring someone else into the chaos, and come out radiant on the other side.

Dedication

I thought long and hard about who I wanted to dedicate this book to, I thought I knew and then changed my mind several more times. I could give the credit to my children. They kept me from going over the cliff many times. I also look back at all the people I crossed paths with. Many of the people I crossed paths with are not worthy of the mention, others absolutely added so much value to my life, but which one. Who has had me my whole life? Who no matter what has always been there good, bad, right, or wrong? The short answer is ME.

I have always been there to pick myself up, learn a better way and move forward. I could always count on me! I would also like to dedicate this book to anyone who has had to pull themselves out of hell, alone. If you have ever noticed your life spiraling out of control in one area or all of them. If you ever woke up one morning and realized, you were somewhere you did not belong. If you ever were living an amazing life one second, and the next it was all gone. To anyone who has realized they have gone too far and needed to find their way back. To anyone that has overcome something meant to destroy them. To anyone who has had more than enough reasons to give up, throw in the towel and end it all, but didn't. To anyone that has felt like they have lost everything and everyone they thought the needed in this life. You are still here, and I see you.

There is no more humbling experience then cleaning up your own mess, whether you caused it yourself or it happened by circumstance. Recovering and rebuilding can be one of the most powerful things you can do, but it is no small task. To heal, grow and evolve, sometimes past friends, family, jobs, and other seasons of our lives is an uphill battle at best. Continuing the good fight, no matter how much the moment sucks when we would rather just crawl in a hole, should be celebrated more. So, if you don't hear it from anyone else, I'll say it. I am so proud of you! You have overcome your demons at least once, are on the hunt for more, and as they say practice makes perfect. The more you do it the easier it becomes. You keep breaking generational curses, overcoming addictions, leaving bad relationships, spreading more love and being true to yourself. Please always remember your people will never be afraid of your light.

Be Loud and speak your truth! I believe in you.

You Grow Darling! They will catch up....... or they won't!

Angel Number 111

A powerful number of manifesting and manifestation. 111 symbolizes enlightenment and a spiritual awakening with high energy, inspiration, and intuition as well as self-expression. You are protected and guided, remember your power now.

Do you not know? Have you not heard? The Lord is the everlasting God, the Creator of the ends of the earth. He will not grow tired or weary, and his understanding no one can fathom. He gives strength to the weary and increases the power of the weak.

– Isaiah 40:28-29 NIV

Chapter 1

Rock Bottom

Have you ever just sat there, at rock bottom, in the middle of your mess, and just wondered why? How? Why did I let this happen? (Maybe again?) How did I follow the same patterns yet another time? And let's not forget those who have hit rock bottom more than once. For me, my mess seems never ending. Just when I think I've got it all figured out, I learn something else about myself that I need to fix or heal. I find a new unhealthy habit or trait that needs my attention. I am a fixer. That is my main coping skill. Well, besides substance abuse. Looking back now on the multiple attempts to stop, and the multiple times I let those down around me. The guilt and shame I carried for a long time, nearly consumed me. No one could ever love me if they knew everything I have done. Why would they want to? That is not the type of person I would want to be around, so I wouldn't blame them one bit! The addiction mindset is a messed-up place to live in. I remember the moment I realized I was an addict; and the moment I realized I was going to detox, on my own, with no help, and be forced to get clean; then the moment after that awful detox when I would actually have to quit the 8 year using habit and be real about my sobriety; And then there is the moment I realized I had to quit using the other substances or coping mechanisms I had put in place of my opiate use that where just as toxic. What a mess.

These moments were not all back-to-back, in fact they are years apart and some more recent than I would like to admit. The point is life will continue to happen, with or without your presence or participation. The only way that I found to keep on the road of recovery is to constantly seek the light, or never quit seeking growth and self-awareness. That doesn't always guarantee you will forever be out of the darkness; bad things will always be a part of the ebb and flow of the universe. But you will always have a better chance of avoiding the darkness if you are already closer to the light. What does that even mean, "Constantly seek the light"? It means look for the good lessons, the positive side, the silver lining. It means during moments of suck, being able to see the bigger picture. It also means being proactive and filling your mind, body, and soul with good and positive things. What you watch, listen too, and surround yourself with matters. Spiritual and religious sources are excellent factors in finding hope, faith, and light. And let's not forget to add what you fuel your body with, intentional body movement (exercise), and a regular sleep schedule is a part of "seeking the light" as well. All of that, plus learning good communication skills so you can understand and build solid relationships with your spouse, children, friends, an extended family. And while you are working on those relationships, you might as well add in your coworkers, job, or business partners in your life. Those relationships are just as important for you to nourish. Wow! No wonder I had a substance abuse problem! That is awful to say I know but come on this is a lot and we can't forget the rest of the things that we have to do just because it is a part of daily maintenance. Things like household chores, paying bills, and any other external issue we oversee handling, all while making sure we always look for the positive in those things too. That is a rough list, and it sounds exhausting.

Especially if you throw any major life event on top of it. Whether they are happy things like getting married, buying a house, having babies, or getting a promotion. Or unhappy things like, cancer, divorce, death, or any other tragedy. What if it's something that you must live with for a while, like an elderly or chronically ill family member? Planning their everyday care or finding someone who can. What if you are left injured and unable to care for yourself after a major tragedy or a devastating diagnosis? Constantly seeking the light during everything can be a struggle but, it is the requirement for a happy and healthy life.

Trust me I had a rough time and mourned the loss of control over this aspect also. It took me years to finally get it right, most of the time, anyway. The truth is we have extraordinarily little control over life events, and I remember when I realized the only thing, I really had control over was me and the behaviors and patterns I had unknowingly picked up from childhood trauma that I had tried to avoid my entire life. Behaviors that had followed me, they were not my fault then, but healing myself now is.

During a Therapy appointment I was tasked with writing a timeline of traumatic events from my childhood. Wow! What an awful homework assignment! I have spent my whole life stuffing that crap deep down to the pits of my soul, so I didn't have to look at it, feel it and certainly not deal with it. I didn't even know if I could remember them all or get them all right. It seemed like there were so many that they just blended together into one big "effed up ball of suck". How could this possibly help? In case you haven't noticed by now, my thought process usually jumps to gloom and doom first, I am a Negative Nancy. I have the amazing ability to see the worst-case scenario, the first time, every-time. Why was the struggle so hard for me to say the things I needed to?

It's a struggle because actually saying exactly what has happened, will be me finally admitting I am a real-life domestic abuse survivor. It makes it known. It applies to me! Don't get me wrong, I am all for talking about Domestic Violence and why it's bad, it should be talked about, and Victims should be able to get the help they need, and I would never hesitate to jump in the middle of a domestic abuse situation if I saw it happening, and I have on a couple of occasions. But in doing so, I am also included in the victim category. It's like I automatically try and void the domestic abuse survivor contract; "I don't really qualify". "My abuse wasn't as bad as I have seen other peoples", "they have it way worse", "I can deal with it". Or it means I have to be brave enough to actually admit I am the girl whose father abandoned her. The girl whose mother was stuck in her own domestic abuse and addiction, with cycles of mess and chaos, and took it out on me, the oldest. I have been an orphan with both parents still alive for most of my life. I must say I suffered from physical, verbal, and mental abuse from my mother, so I subconsciously continued to put myself in similar situations, to repeat the cycle of abuse, ever since. It's what I know, it's comforting.

She never searched for help, admitted her faults, apologized for taking it out on me or did anything to make me feel like I was a loved and wanted child. I had to walk away from my mother and prevent her from being in my children's lives due to her toxic behavior. I had to break the cycle. If she were not going to seek the light and find her way, I could no longer tolerate her destruction in my life. As much as I tried my whole life to be different, I realize now I repeated many of the things she did. Some things I did better, but others I did not. Wow. So many things I have been carrying, that were not even mine to carry. I never really dealt with the trauma I witnessed and lived through, and I went through life assuming every person, who got close, would treat me the same. I have a huge fortress built around me so no one can get close enough to hurt me. I know I am getting ahead of myself, first my timeline.

Facing the reality of all my shadows, saying "Yes, I lived through this, and because of it I am determined to find something else, and become something better." The problem with childhood trauma, is we usually don't know enough at the time to realize these are not lessons we needed to learn and there are other ways of life and coping skills that don't involve numbing yourself, yelling, screaming, hitting, throwing things, manipulation or causing fear. Hell, it took me well into adulthood to realize I had an anger problem and no real coping skills. And then I was angry about that! Like why did no one tell me that I didn't really have to fight the whole way through my teenage and young adult years? What was I fighting for anyway? Why was I so angry and determined to make it despite of? What did I really need or want? The little girl in me just wanted to be heard and accepted for the good girl she wanted so desperately to be.

I had no idea how to be a normal functioning mom or wife. I didn't know what a happy and healthy woman even looked like. This was going to be an interesting journey. I didn't know what I needed, but I knew I needed something different. I was ready to accept whatever that was.

Angel Number 211

A reminder to you that balance is the goal. Pay attention to your thoughts and feelings to the subtle and strong vibrations that you emit and surround yourself with for they play a huge role in creating your reality. Embrace transformation. Let go of the old so we can welcome the new.

I will be a father to him, and he'll be a son to me. When he does wrong, I'll discipline him in the usual ways, the pitfalls, and obstacles of the mortal life. But I will never remove my gracious love from him. – **2 Samuel 7:14-15**

Chapter 2

Daddy Issues

F irst up in my timeline of doom, is where all my daddy issues lay. I was incredibly young when my dad "left". My father was never really in the picture. He lived in another state and rarely made an effort, unless the wife he was currently with was interested in a step-daughter. I learned from him to never count on a man. Men will tell you one thing and do another. That seems harsh, I know. I would imagine that it isn't at the top of the list of things men hope they pass on to their little girls. At least I know it's not for most of the men I try to surround myself with today, but at the time, he was the first man that was supposed to make me feel unconditional love. My daddy, my hero. I don't pretend to know his situation or why he made the choices he made. In my travels through Grace, I have learned that regardless of the choices he did or did not make, whether he was in my life or not, his choices had everything to do with him and his struggle with healing, and nothing to do with me or who I am. My perception of men at the time, and for a long time in my life, was "men couldn't be trusted". I treated all men the same and expected the same out of all of them.

As a toddler I remember a big physical fight involving my dad, and future stepdad. I was later told the fight was because my dad was sexually molesting me, so my new stepdad beat him up for it. I believed that story my whole life. I never felt any fear around my dad at any time, until he met my children for the first time. Whether I believed it or not, I still subconsciously watched for the signs when he was around them. It's not like we ever had a real meaningful relationship either way. I only saw him on special occasions like big holidays and funerals. Interesting enough, at some point I had accepted that I was sexually molested by my dad, only to be asked how I knew that later in life. "Do You have any memories?" I was asked by a therapist in my early 20's. Well, no, I just remember the fight between my father and future stepfather. So, is it more likely my mother lied to me? I didn't believe that then, but looking back now? It's plausible. No matter which way you look at it, it's an effed-up situation. Either my dad sexually molested me around the age of one or two, or my mother lied about it. If she lied, I believe it might have been to get custody or make me love her more because she protected me. It's just more proof of how our unhealed parts can hurt those around us. Why was their fighting and B.S. my responsibility to hold on to anyway? Whatever my dad was dealing with then or now, and considering I have had to walk away from my own mother too, maybe he needed to run as well. Maybe he needed to get far away from her or vice versa? It took him another 4-6 marriages before he found his true love, and Jesus. Either way, I am well into my adult life and there still has not been much effort on my dad's part. Hopefully, he really is doing better now, but somehow, I just "know", he still has got some work to do. It's a process that I am learning still and have not gotten completely right either.

My daddy issues made me constantly seek attention from men because at a very young age I needed that validation and never got it. I needed that presence in my life so desperately because I never had it. And let's face it, I didn't seek it in the healthiest of ways. I had no idea what I was missing, I just knew it was missing. I needed to find the perfect person to fill that void! Unfortunately, no one ever told me that what I was searching for could never be fulfilled by someone else. I chased feelings for a long time. When the feelings faded or the honeymoon stage passed, that was my sign it was not real, and I needed to bounce. Just like the addict I would eventually become, I was searching for the quick fix, instant gratification, and lust. I repeated this cycle multiple times, before I finally figured it out.

Angel Number 311

311 is the number of development in every area of your life. When this number appears, it is a sure sign change is coming. This is your reminder – you must promise yourself a better future, keep dreaming about it as you go through the testy transition period. Greatness is within you.

Her Children rise up and call her blessed; her husband also, and he praises her: 'Many women have done excellently, but you surpass them all.' – **Proverbs 31:28-31**

Chapter 3

Mommy Issues

The list of trauma and suck runs way deeper here. Naturally, my mother was my primary caregiver for most of my childhood life. She used to say she broke the generational curse because she stopped hitting us. Her logic is she was beat by her dad and her mother never stopped it. She had emotional, verbal, and physical domestic violence in her home. She said the physical was worse on her. She told me it was because you couldn't hide the physical effects of actual beatings, everyone would know for sure then. She was tough enough to let the words that would crush anyone's soul run off her back and not phase her. Well, that is what she wants you to believe. She thought that breaking the generational curse was ONE thing, physical violence. The reality of it is that breaking the curse means not subjecting your children to ALL the things that could cause childhood trauma, not just one thing. After all the things that I have witnessed, felt, or dealt with, she should have prevented or at least tried to. She was so hyper focused on one thing that she missed a million little things. Being so focused on one behavior and not acknowledging the other patterns of abuse is still repeating abusive behavior. I blamed her for messing me up for a long time. I felt cheated because I missed out on having a real mother, a nurturing and caring one. Because of the lack of nurturing and a mother's love, I had not learned healthy coping skills in life or real communication skills. To compare it to how I felt, it's like a toddler being thrown into a pool as means to teach them to swim. It can be done, but at what cost? It's traumatizing for the toddler, but they learn to swim, right? So, was harm done to the toddler or not? Perception is everything here.

No one taught me the correct way to negotiate or ask for what I needed. I was not required to check myself or control my emotions in my teenage and young adult years. Well, that was the behavior that my mom modeled for me. I learned the pattern and inevitably created it in my life for a long time. I held onto what happened to me in my younger years and hid it from everyone out of guilt and shame. "What will people think of me if they knew?" The Bible tells us to honor our mother and father. How do you honor someone who hurt you if you are only speaking the truth? How can I protect my children from repeating the cycle if I can't talk about it? Do I stay silent or bring all the shadows to the light?

This timeline was a real struggle for me to put into words, but once I started writing, things just poured out. I like to write, and I tossed the idea around about writing a book for so long. I started and stopped my writing more times than I can count. I love a good empowerment book about people going through real struggle and coming out on top! More specifically kids from the wrong side of the streets, or people who go from having nothing, to completely building and changing their life or doing something different and bam! They make all their dreams come true or achieved something awesome! Hmmm... I wonder why? I was looking for ways to get to the things and places that brought me peace and joy so that I can finally feel like I belonged somewhere.

I remembered why I stopped being real in my writing, I used to journal every day. I would talk to my diary like my best friend. I would share the good and the ugly of everyday life. Until one day my mom found it, read it, and then screamed at me for writing certain things. That if I write anything down it becomes permanent! "People will use that against you later in life!" Looking back, I can see the coping skills she learned. I was just trying to find a good outlet, and I wasn't allowed to do so. We kept secrets and didn't talk about the bad stuff. No one could know the truth behind the walls.

I tried to write here and there after that, but I could never get anything real, until now. What else did I see? What other memories affect me now without me truly knowing? Another one popped in my head; I watched my mom get caught shoplifting expensive shampoo and conditioner. That was an awful experience, she was crying and begging, and I remembered thinking "this is when they are going to finally take me away from her." I was so scared and afraid of the bad people they will stick me with! We all new those stories of foster care and orphanages! "We may have it bad, but those kids have it worse", I thought. We were still given toys and presents when we were good or at

Christmas time. None of that would happen in "those places."
I was younger, so I would not have understood what was really happening, but I know the police showed up, asked a bunch of questions, did their part and eventually we were allowed to leave.

It is hard to keep going here. There seems to be a never-ending supply of effed-up experiences that I don't want to pass on to my children, but somehow, I'm sure, I already have in some ways. That was a hard realization for me! That in uncovering the things my mom did that messed me up, I had done some of the same, unknowingly, in front of my own children. I may never know if they really understood what was happening or not. I have always been upfront with them about bad things I have done when given the opportunity. Depending on the topic or questions and ages, I think I offer more advice than they needed or wanted at certain times. I guess it was my way of making sure they knew I was here and would help them with anything. But mostly I had those conversations in hopes that they would make a better choice, some things I didn't really realize I needed to change, until my 30's. So, while some of my bad habits are easier to fix in my younger kids, I have already "messed up" my older ones. How do I correct it now? The voice in my head tells me to "keep talking."

There was always fighting, drama, cheating, and drugs. My mom and stepdad had a very violent relationship. They beat the crap out of each other all the time. It usually ended with someone getting hurt and needing to go to the hospital or one of them getting arrested. When the fighting started, my sisters and I would run and hide. It was my job to round them up and take them to safety. It was just two of us for a while, before our baby sister came into the mix. We had a couple of places we could go, depending on where the fight was. The Christmas Tree was always our favorite. We would hide underneath and look at the lights until it was safe to come out. There were times, though, when we all had to escape. We would run upstairs to Grandma's part of the house and go straight to her bedroom. Her room was the only room with a lock and access to the roof, so we can escape. My stepdad was super handy, though. He always had ladders and tools lying around, so we would lock ourselves in the bedroom, climb out the window and mom would jump off the roof, holding my little sister, and put the ladder up for me so we could all get to safety. We would sleep out in the car, usually across the street in the court or another parking lot. I remember a few times when it was cold, and we got to go to hotels.

One time we got to stay in a suite because the heat in our regular room didn't work! I guess all my stories are not so bad, I sure felt like royalty that night in that huge fancy room! The memory of the fancy hotel is quickly replaced by other bad ones though. Another memory is one where we had finally gotten away to the safety of our hotel, but mom HAD to call him. This was back in the day when each time you dialed out you had to pay a fee to be connected. (I know, some real Stone Age stuff, right?) They were still fighting after we were free, then she walked away from the phone. My logical child brain told me to hang it up, solve the problem…. goodbye! Can you imagine how that ended for me? I think that was the last time she beat me. I can't be certain, but I know that night she went overboard. I feel like there was one more thing that really stands out in my mind before we move to after the birth of my littlest sister. I know I testified in court a lot for things, but I don't necessarily remember what they were all for. Was it all just custody things? Or were they more along the lines of events like the time my little sister and I were in the back seat, when my mother and my stepdad stopped at a red light, got out of the car, and walked back to a couple in a fancy red convertible behind us? My mom punched the girl, my stepdad punched the guy, they both got back in the car and drove off like nothing happened. Who really knows, but either way I was always conditioned and primed on what I was allowed to say and what I was not allowed to say in the court of law.

No, now I remembered more! There was another incident where mom and I were locked out of my stepdad's mother's house. We were trying to get back in the house to get our things, but my stepdad and his mom had used a 2X4 to make sure no one could open the front door. It was a split-level foyer when you walked in, so, they had the 2X4 wedged between the landing and the door so even though we could unlock the door we still couldn't get in. We had a huge privacy fence around our backyard. My job was to climb the fence and see if I could get in the back door. Stepdad's car was not home, and the house looked pretty dark and empty, so we figured it would be safe. When I got to the back door, to my surprise, my stepdad was waiting for me. I was petrified. He told me to get back into the car, so I turned and walked back to the fence and opened the gate. My mom asked if I got in, but she knew something was wrong by the expression of pure fear and panic on my face. I got back in the car while they fought for a few minutes. Mom got in the car and rolled up her window. My stepdad had an old-school tape recorder in his hands. Apparently, he tapped the phone line and didn't like her conversations. As mom started to drive off, and my stepdad swung the tape recorder and busted out the driver side window. All of the glass flew over to my side, landing on me and cutting me. I was probably around 9 years old at the time. An ambulance was called, and the paramedics picked glass out of me at the end of the street, but I wasn't allowed to go to the hospital. Mom refused medical treatment, but the cops allowed us to go into the house and get our belongings. Celebrate the little victories.

We moved again shortly after, this time into our own house with my stepdad. Apparently, all their problems would disappear if they just got away from Grandma. So that is just what we did. I was excited to have my own room and some positive change. Though in the end, it really didn't happen the way I had hoped.

We were always investigating something, looking for license plates and certain people out to get us or whatever the real story was. I didn't understand why all these people were out to get us. What were we really looking for? I remember there were multiple times I helped my mother spy on people and in return we caught plenty spying on us.

My mom and stepdad ended up going through a separation, so it quickly turned into his people keeping tabs on her and her people keeping tabs on him, but I wonder, if there was more to it. I was older now and considered more responsible, but I started smoking cigarettes around this time of being "more responsible", as well as becoming the constant caretaker for my little sisters. Mom worked 3rd shift and my stepdad was gone, so I always had my little sisters while mom slept, went out, or worked. I made dinner on a regular basis which consisted of a lot of Ramen noodles or things I could put in the microwave. There were other guys that came and went during this time, one of them started coming around more and more, until my stepdad caught them together, which quickly escalated.

I heard his voice and knew something violent was about to happen. I quickly herded the kids upstairs while the next world war began. The fight between them was taken outside. There was a small window at the landing of the steps where I could see a little bit of the fight. My stepdad had a shovel and started beating the new boyfriend's truck and then turned the shovel toward the new boyfriend. My mom quickly inserted herself between her men. The fight headed towards the stairs leading to the house and out of my sight, when I heard my mom Scream "OH MY GOD WHAT DID YOU DO?" I ran down to the side door to investigate and found my mom hysterical, my stepdad kneeling on the ground, holding his stomach. I could see blood was everywhere. I don't know why or how I knew what to do, but I ran and grabbed some towels and threw them at my stepdad, so he could apply pressure to his wounds, and then I called 911. The rest of that night is a blur, but the aftermath was worse. Her new boyfriend stabbed my stepdad 3 times, coming close to ending his life and then ran to a fire station around the block to turn himself in. My stepdad was in intensive care for two weeks and the media followed us everywhere! We were finally celebrities. Not exactly what I was hoping for when we moved into the new place. It was also revealed that my mother's boyfriend was 17, while I was only about to be 14.

We moved again shortly after the stabbing with another

guy who was also "just a friend". There was less drama, but more partying during this time. There were always people over our house drinking and smoking weed, but I had noticed that mom always had a lot of prescription bottles as well. They were fun times though. Music was always playing with people dancing, and I got to play DJ by picking songs and rewinding the cassette tapes. Yes, more Stone Age stuff, I know. This didn't last long, though. The new boyfriend drama and stepdad stalking us continued. We had to move again, this time to Pennsylvania. Mom's new boyfriend almost moved with us, but we got our own place instead. I don't know if he got cold feet or if it was divine intervention that stopped that one, but I'll take the blessing. We moved into the new place with just me and my mom because my sisters had to stay with their dad. Since I wasn't his natural daughter, I had to say with my mom, away from my sisters. Quickly, other "friends" started to come and go. Without my sisters, I was alone again. This was the time in my life that I had given up and started not caring, fighting back against the tumultuous life I was subjected to with my mom. Having the ability to care for my sisters when mom wouldn't, was the only thing at the time that held me together. I remember struggling to avoid making my mom mad at first, because she was a loose cannon. I was a normal teenager though, and I didn't always do the right things though I really was a good kid. I desperately wanted to make my mother happy, so I would clean the house, do the dishes or some random chore and then wait for her to come home. I would be all excited waiting for her reaction. Finally, this would be the time she would walk in, get a big smile, and tell me how proud of me she was. Maybe I would even get a big hug and thank you, I hoped. Nope. She would always find something wrong with what I did. I had messed something up or didn't do something the exact right way she wanted. I was damned if I did and damned if I didn't. She was going to yell at me whether I was bad or good, so I might as well do what I wanted. Either way I was going to get the same reaction from her, so what did it matter? I was done listening to her or caring what she thought. So, I became a rebel without a cause.

I continued my people pleasing in other ways and found myself jumping on the substance abuse train. I was out of control. I skipped school and did whatever I wanted. My mother would drop me off at school and watch me walk in the front door, but I would just keep going and walk right out the back door. I was choosing not to study or play a sport anymore. I tried that in 5th and 6th grade. I was on a Softball team, I loved it and I was good at it. In one year, I had moved up to fast pitch softball where we could steal bases, I was good at that too. Unfortunately, this was before my stepdad was stabbed, so once we moved to PA and I had to give up my teammates, I was already heading in the wrong direction, with no one to pull me back.

My mom continued to work 3rd shift and provided me with a babysitter. The babysitter happened to also be my mother's best friend at the time. Since I liked to sneak out while she was away, her best friend was the perfect choice to watch over me. The babysitter would wake me up in the middle of the night so that I could blow into this thing in her car that would allow her to start it. She needed me to blow into it so she could run to a friend's house. I would sleep in the car, and she would just wake me up when I needed to blow. Sounds like an awesome role model, right? Thank God for His protection that night as I stayed in the car, on the side the road of who- knows-where, while my babysitter grabbed her fix. She borrowed a dollar from me when we got home to seal the deal, as payment for blowing in that thing for her. All these things add up and took a toll on me after a while.

At 14 years old I attempted to take my own life, leaving a note behind. My first real boyfriend and I had broken up, but I couldn't honestly tell you why. We were both teenagers going down the wrong path. Again, I was left loveless and desperate for my pain to stop. My mother had a pharmacy in the house, so I picked a bottle that had a lot in it and counted them. I took 47 amitriptyline tablets that night. I am grateful now that my mom found me instead of dying. Apparently, I had fell off the bed, which caused a big thud and she came running to find me unconscious. She called 911 and I made it to the hospital. I had my stomach pumped and woke up the next morning in the hospital. After a week's stay at a psych ward, because I was clearly suicidal, no real changes in my mental health occurred, but I was allowed to go back home. I knew the stories I would need to tell them in order to get out of the hospital. I'd been conditioned for "the system". My rebellion continued on.

After my rebellion escalated, and I physically attacked my mother during an argument, the state stepped in. I was on drugs and I was just done with mom treating me the way she did, telling me what to do. I had so much anger and rage built up inside! Her boyfriend at the time handed me a beating a few days later that sent me to the hospital, just to get back at me for attacking my mom. As soon as I went to the hospital, I was immediately sent back into "the system". I deserved the bruises I got that day, but the hospital sent me to a shelter because they thought I was the victim. Shortly into my shelter stay, they realized it was me that was out of control. My mom was getting fines for my skipping school, and there was a paper trail of trouble already building against me.

The Marietta House in Lancaster, Pennsylvania was my new home. I quickly became part of a minority there and learned to shut my big mouth, quick! (The same big mouth I was not afraid to use in my hometown). I was "bigger" there, my mom couldn't even control me. In this house I was one of only two or three other white girls that passed through during my stay, but that was it! I was 16 and never really knew a person of any other race. At that time my area was mostly Caucasian or Mexican. Mom always said, 'in this family, we are not allowed to date black people." She said it was because our extended family in Ohio would disown us. Of course, that intrigued me, and scared me at the same time. In this house, I found myself in very unfamiliar territory, I was on my best behavior. I never spoke unless spoken to and stayed in my shell. I listened though, very intently. I was a sponge, and I was waiting for the worst stuff to start happening. Funny thing was it never did. I loved it at this house and I actually excelled because of the structure. I joined lots of clubs at my new diverse school, JP McCaskey High School. Joining the clubs got me out of the house to experience a whole new world. I was even elected Vice President of one of the clubs! I made real connections, met so many amazing and different people. At the house, my walls came down and the girls became my sisters. I can truly say that time was one of the happier times of my childhood. (Forget that I was court ordered to be locked up in placement for troubled girls) What is the common denominator between the time I spent in the house and now? Short answer- Faith, self-love, and removal of the toxic environment.

I went to church every Sunday with whoever the staff was that day. So for 6 months of lock up, I got to go to a diverse group of churches. I wish I could remember the names of the churches. I remember going to one church that was just like going to the movies! It was a little white church with about 20-30 pews. There were a few steps in the front of the church, leading to an alter with a Jesus statue and big king like chair. The people in the church were all African American, all but me! I was so excited to just soak it all up! They sang the best songs and danced with the most passion I'd ever seen! I swear this little old man who had to be 90-years old, got up out of the King's Chair with the beat of the music and danced his way down the aisle, as if a miracle had just happened! It was the best!

Another one of my favorite churches was the complete opposite of the last. It was a huge, well-lit, wide-open church. This one was mostly Caucasian. There was a huge stage with cameras everywhere! "For a TV show", I thought. I felt like I was in a famous church. There was a digital screen there that would call parents to come get their assumingly bad kids. When everyone sang, they got up and danced to the beat of the electric guitar players, I didn't even know guitars were allowed in church! It's funny to look back at this "famous church" now that I'm older. I loved the church so much I was Saved the day with the guitars, at the age of 16. It was a truly powerful moment, even though I didn't fully understand what being "saved" meant, it just felt right. I went to many other churches, and I truly loved each of them.

From the moment I was "saved", I decided I was going to be Spiritual! It didn't matter to me what religion or section of the Church you are from; God's message is the same. The meaning behind each sermon whether it was Catholic, Baptist's, Lutheran, Methodist, Presbyterian, Church of Christ or whatever, the sermons always hit home. Each time I walked through the door of the church, whether I was a member of it or not., I felt welcomed and I felt peace in my heart, whatever the topic was. It is my personal relationship with God that matters the most to me. The message that was delivered was always meant for me in that moment. I felt highly loved and favored in those moments. I wish I could have bottled them up so I could have them ready for all the dark moments that came after.

Trying to fit back into a world I didn't want to go back to after lock-up was scary. I got out a little early, for good behavior, and I didn't want to be the ass I was before. In high school, I couldn't go preaching that the Holy Spirit got me! Thank God it was my senior year, right? I thought, "I just have to get through the rest of this year, then I can be who I was really born to be!", whoever that was. It's hard to comprehend when you're young how big the world is and how many options you really do have.

I would love to tell you, I learned my lesson this time and that I came home a changed teenager, never to be bad again, but that is not where my troubles ended. HA! I almost chuckle now, to think of how much extra pain and discomfort I created for myself over the years by just reacting badly. I quickly jumped back into old habits. Thankfully, I managed to graduate high school. I was book smart and got decent grades without even trying hard or showing up half the time. Right after graduation, life threw me another curveball that shocked my system, but it gave me a little more clarity.

Angel Number 411

This Number is a message of support and encouragement. 411 tells us to be patient and respectful towards people in our life because we all depend on each other's help. Practicing positive thinking and having a little faith is the perfect combination for succeeding in life.

For this child I prayed, and the Lord has granted me the desires of my heart.

1 Samuel 1:27

Chapter 4

New Mom

The birth of my first daughter gave me new meaning. Brooklyn Makaye Isaac was born April 16th, 2004. It was a little after 4pm when she blessed my world. She is brilliant and beautiful! I honestly wonder how I got so lucky to be her momma. I was 19 years old and had no clue what I was doing in life. I wanted to be a mom so bad! Her father and I had met only a few months before I got pregnant, but the relationship ended with cheating and betrayal before she was born. He popped back in and out of our lives a few times, until he finally exited stage left and never popped backed up. Even though our relationship didn't work out, my heart broke for my daughter. I knew what it felt like not to be:

chosen". I decided to stop messing around with partying when my daughter was around and I did my best to focus only on her. She was so tiny and sweet and perfect. I was determined to figure it all out for her sake. She was everything I ever wanted. I feel like I got a lot of it wrong anyway, especially after she was born. My mom would help me with daycare while I worked, but in every other aspect of her young life, I was determined to raise her myself. I still lived with my mother though and she made it more difficult for us all. My intentions were always great, but boy, I didn't have a clue. I gave up a lot of what I had in order to open up my heart and be the mom I wanted to become for her. The one I never had. It was going to be easy, because I knew exactly what I was not going to do!

Oh, Come on! I know you have thought that one before! "I will do better than, (insert the name that comes to mind here) because I WON'T do what He/She did!" Sound familiar? Unfortunately, I learned there is more of a right or wrong side then there is a right and wrong answer. Each side has many options or paths to choose from. Can you guess, who is great at finding more wrong ways to do something? Yes, you guessed it! ME! This would have been an excellent time for me to tap into some of that bottled up Self Love and Faith from the church I mentioned.

I couldn't live with my mom's aggression and feel like I was a good mom at the same time, so I made the decision to move out of her house. She was just so mean, negative, and degrading all the time. If she wasn't gossiping about someone, she was trying to control someone or something else or trying to manipulate whatever she could to get what she wanted. She only cared about herself. Me, my daughter, and two other friends of mine got an apartment together so we could all split the rent, making it easier on everyone. Once we settled in, I started going to college for my RN. I was going to create a better life for me and Brooklyn no matter how hard it was. Unfortunately, I continued down the wrong path in my relationships. Subconsciously, I must have been searching for unconditional love and unlimited desire. The problem is, as I said earlier, I was searching for a feeling. I spent years looking for something that is completely unobtainable. I wish I would have asked myself "how do you expect to find and maintain a feeling, forever?", or "do you realize how ridiculous you sound right now?" How about, "you should spend some time with you and learn to love yourself first!", "Focus on making yourself a better woman and the rest will absolutely fall into place", "believe in yourself!" Did I say any of that to myself? No. Did I have anyone in my life saying, "Girl you need to find you and date you for a while?" Again, No. Instead, I cycled through another toxic relationship, and another daughter, repeating the same behavior, but in a slightly different cycle. It was always slightly different but never far off.

I met another guy and moved in with him and his parents. That should have been my first red flag, but I loved that house and it felt amazing to have a somewhat normal family. The relationship between us turned out to be more toxic than not. This one was another serial cheater and liar. I got pregnant fast, but he was already cheating, and I was stuck. I lived with him and his parents, and now I was going to add another baby into the mix. I felt like I just couldn't do it, I couldn't have another baby now. Brooklyn was only 6 months old, and I was going to be a single mother to 2 babies? How could I bring another baby into our lives when I could barely support the one I had? So, I secretly had an abortion. I felt like the world's worst person. I hated myself for a long time, and those thoughts still creep up from time to time. (This is where the murder commandment is broken, for those of you waiting for that part!)

I was empty and heartbroken again. I ended it with the boyfriend and moved back in with mom. I found out he was going to jail anyway, for something he had done before he met me. Just like his cheating lies, he kept this from me too. More red flags!

I ended up jumping back to a relationship with a lifelong guy friend of mine. I knew he loved me and would do anything for me, and I knew he came from a great family. He could provide too! We decided were going to move in together, but his parents insisted we get married. So, against my better judgement, we got married, and spent the whole day fighting. On our wedding day, I showed up to the courthouse in jeans. It was the most awkward Wedding Day ever. (More red flags anyone?) We got an apartment together, but after a month it was turning violent. I wanted so bad to get away from my mother and get my daughter out of that house that I would do almost anything to get away. I never learned to run to something better, I just turned to anything that was available, so I went back to moms and took back the last guy. He did his time in jail, but he assured me he was a "changed man". I got pregnant again and I knew I was unable to support another child right now, but I couldn't have another abortion either. I would have to make it work. So, I quit RN school and started working at Kay Jewelers.

Lexus Morgan Isaac decided to come flying out January 12, 2007 and has not slowed down since. She is my free-spirited lover. There is nothing she wouldn't do for anyone in need, she just loves everyone. She is also an amazing cook! I thank her grandmother for that. Plus, she teaches me now too, win-win!

When my relationship with her dad ended, because of his cheating again, I moved back into moms. This time we moved into an apartment she made in the attic. I would have my own space with my kids, I was excited! In the meantime, I applied for low-income housing and was on the 6-month waiting list.

I was bound and determined to do things better, quicker, and different this time. I had been here before, I knew this life, how can I do it easier and faster this time? It didn't take me long to snap out of that cycle and create a new one. I needed a new plan, a new way, a new type. Thinking back, they always cheated and I always left. This was my cycle of learned repeated behavior; from both my personal past experiences and the ones I watched my parents go through. Do you ever feel like you repeat the same cycles over and over? We try so hard to do things different, and it still ends up being the same cycle just in a slightly different package. Right? I found tons of the wrong side of things and very few right sides.

I added more responsibility and less time for self-love. When did it become normal to say things such as, "I have been hurt by past relationships, so I have to be careful", instead of "this person really hurt me and I should never allow that person to do it again". Create the boundary with the hurtful person or act, not with every person that represents the possibility of the dream! You know the dream! Whichever story you play over and over in your head about the type of relationship you want. Goodness, that is much easier said than done, I know. For me it goes something like this, we will go on a date or two and there will be an instant connection. Our eyes meet, that spark ignites between us, and the flames of passion will burn deep and forever. I will be the perfect wife and mom, he will love all of me all the time and my kids will be so grateful.   Everyone will adore me. Is this just my story? Looking back, I certainly had a warped idea of love. The problem is I was killing myself everything I felt I needed to do to achieve that special kind of love. I never thought anyone would want to be with me if I couldn't provide them something. Money, attention, time, performing housewife tasks or duties, sex, etc. I put so much pressure on myself, for a long time after this too, never realizing it. I would get burnt out and resentful very quickly into my relationships. These guys were all the same! Please tell me you see how I kept getting more of the same! I was still looking for my validation elsewhere. Someone else had to give me my meaning and purpose. I needed to receive unconditional love from someone else. Boy, was I way off in my thinking.

I had two babies at the age of 21 to support as a single woman. I wasn't necessarily a single mom because their grandparents where very much around for the girls and me. Their dad's where around here and there as well, it really does take a village. It's just as lonely as a single woman, but a slightly different kind of lonely then a single mom. When you're a single woman, you're alone to entertain yourself when your children are with the other parent. That is no simple task when you don't love yourself. We don't look to fill those times with good nurturing thoughts or activities, do we? Chances are these moments are the ones filled with ice cream and tears, sleeping or just being so filled with anxiety you have to somehow numb the pain. I struggled to be alone with my own thoughts. I constantly felt like a failure unless I had some great accomplishment happening or close to happening. I needed validation and recognition from someone. I needed to know I was on the right path, doing good work, or at least on the right hemisphere. I partied when I didn't have the girls but when I did, I tried to spend as much quality time with them as I could.

I did hold true to picking a different breed of guy the next time though. I had learned to be a powerhouse too. It was my destiny, right? I could prove how strong I really am, and I could wear that strength as a badge of Honor. I would get the validation one way or another. Maybe my personality was too strong, I needed to find someone who wouldn't react to me and escalate to a relationship that was volatile, someone that could teach me to calm down and trust. Insert my 2nd ex-husband, he did just that.

Angel Number 511

This number suggests that some karmic life changes are ahead of you right now. Your Angels want you to remain courageous and cheerful throughout these transitions. They support you with love and healing. Make time for yourself and trust your intentions will manifest.

But each person is tempted when is lured and enticed by his own desire. Then desire when it has conceived gives birth to sin and sin when fully grown brings forth death. – **James 1:14-15**

Chapter 5

The Calm Before The Storm

I will forever be grateful for the next man, because he has taught me so much about life and myself over our 10 years together. It felt like a lifetime because our relationship had an impactful life and death that was mourned, but necessary.

I have said it before, many times, he was "exactly what I needed at the time". He was the calm to my storm and he was safe (I was desperate to finally feel safe), I made most of the deciding factors, later in life learning it was more for my need to control something then to just make better choices. It was never a power struggle, just the natural order of our house. I was a hot head; everyone knew it, and no one questioned it. He was patient and understanding and I was a spitfire that reacted. I would like to think I gave him a good 3 years before my old habits came roaring back. Old habits I had worked so hard to break. Looking back now, I was a nightmare to live with. I don't know how or why he stayed and put up with my crap for so long.

I have struggled recalling memories of our fights. They rarely happened and I took it as a sign I had finally gotten it right. I accused him in the beginning of cheating like the rest, but he never reacted, he would just hand me his phone. I was able to check anything at any time if I ever questioned anything he was doing. I eventually stopped asking and learned to trust him. He had calmed me down. The pregnancy of our son was planned, I had done something else right! I was actually married, and we were having our first son together.

My first baby boy made his appearance March 30, 2010. Trenton Mitchell Harrell was my biggest baby and definitely a momma's boy. He is my sweet, caring, little lover always thinking about others first. I am also impressed by his cooking skills! After Trenton joined us, I took the full 12 weeks off that my job allowed for maternity leave. At that time, I thought my son was going to be my last baby, so, I stayed home and soaked up the baby snuggles. I enjoyed being a stay-at-home momma with my babies. It was a nice break in my normal routine. During the time I was on maternity leave, I was also in a huge custody battle with my oldest daughters' father, who is also the brother of my current husband. Yes, I warned you my life was quite the train wreck. My current husband and I just became outnumbered by children. Yes, the odds were already against me, and my mental health. Still, I was trucking along trying to be the best version of me I knew to be at the time. I was struggling, but I kept pushing forward.

Before I dive into this section, I must first acknowledge, that my addictions were at their peak, my recollection and perception of these events are cloudy at best. The lessons I pulled from this time period helped to make me who I am today. Though I'm not proud of my past actions, I'm no longer ashamed they happened. I trust and believe I have guilt-tripped and shamed myself more than anyone else ever could about my poor decision-making skills for my entire life. So, without further ado, my timeline of doom continues.

I went back to work after 12 weeks of snuggling the baby on the couch. I jumped right back into lifting and maneuvering people as a CNA and earned myself three Herniated disks in my lower back with excruciating pain down both my legs and into my feet. The spiral of my addiction started here. This was at a time when it was normal to be prescribed Opiates for pain. I was given seven, yes seven, 5mg Percocet's a day to start. Wow! I was a Happy Camper then, but to look back now, what a disservice that doctor did for me.

When I went back to work, I jumped back into my people pleasing at work and at home, until I quickly became burnt out. This was during the beginning of my career in the medical field. The lifting and maneuvering of patients as a CAN was a lot for me. I needed to move up the food chain so I could have a less physically demanding job, so I enrolled in a one-year accelerated Licensed Practical Nursing program starting the following January.

Now, I liked to partake in drugs, so I did them whenever they were available, "responsibly" but it was not daily and they didn't interfere with other aspects of my life, but my addiction quickly grew out of control once I hurt myself. I felt better at first, with no pain. I could handle all the things that a busy nursing student, mom of three, fighting a custody battle and being a fabulous wife could handle. If I just had those meds.

For a while I was killing it. At life, at home, at work, at school, Then I started running out of the pills sooner than I was supposed to, so I needed to supplement with something else. My doctor started to catch on that I had an issue with the pills, since he had already upped my monthly amount to cover 14 pills a day. The pain meds were controlling me now. No one knew, no one could find out. I made excuses, stole from work, family, and people that I loved in order to nurse and feed my addiction. I did it all while maintaining life, pretending to be a functioning member of society. I became someone I didn't recognize and most definitely didn't want to be. Because I was running out of pills sooner than I was supposed to, the withdrawal intensified the pain I already had. My entire body would scream at me when I didn't have the pain pills. On top of the pain, now I realized the pills made me feel more pain than I actually had, so I would need more. I also had that negative Nancy brain and horrible thoughts to contend with. The pills were always my priority. I had to make sure I had enough to get me through today and tomorrow, because if I had them, I could kill it at life. If I didn't, I spent the day hunting.... or sick. What have I become? I didn't discriminate either, opiates were my thing, but I was a trash can. Anything was better than nothing, and who cares about mixing? I'd take anything I could get my hands on to avoid full withdrawal. There were times I ended up scoring enough pain pills for a week and wondered if it was better to stretch them out over the week, or just take them all and stop the cycle of addiction. My heart breaks for that woman now. How broken she was and had been her whole life, just trying to escape the pain.

I remember admitting to my husband I had a problem and needed help. He held onto my bottle to help me wean down. He had gone through a similar situation a few years earlier, but it didn't take him long to bounce back. Me? I already had a tolerance built up. My addiction continued to grow out of control and coupled with an addictive personality, it didn't take much for me to get hooked. I was crafty though, I found the bottle and told him I was good. I had it under control, and I was done. I lied, and he never questioned me again, still to this day. I really feel like he was so scared of my reaction he stayed quiet. I hated the person I had become, I stayed on the couch most of the time.

My reactions were out of control, I was the abuser here. I had thought he calmed me down, he didn't. It was just that he never reacted to me. I had no one to fight with but myself.

My mother was still in my life then, but I had kept her at arm's length. I could see the aggression in her but not what I had learned from her. I failed to recognize the anger and hurt I carried still. I was still fighting even though I was safe from her and I didn't even know it.

The Next stage, I would never wish on my worst enemy, ever. If you have been through withdrawal, I would imagine you would agree. I have heard and seen plenty of withdrawing patients, and knew the process, but feeling it is a whole other level. I call this next section my living death. Have you ever felt like you truly died and then had to wake up the next day and still go on? After death you are supposed to get some relief in Heaven, right? I died every night and had to get up to do it all over again the next day, for months, while no one knew.

I remembered the actions I took to be cut off from my doctor. How warped my thought process was to think this was a great idea. He had caught on to my addiction and planned to taper me back but gave me my prescription early again. This time he dated the script for Monday, but this was a Friday and I had already been out. I was desperate. I altered the prescription and tried my best at the pharmacy. They didn't fill it and I was placed on a no treat list. I was done, cut off, no more pills freely coming in. I had to accept defeat and prepare for getting through withdrawal. I had wanted to anyway, deep down inside, but could never actually bring myself to do it on my own. Until now, I was being forced. Thank God I was a powerhouse. When Britni gets backed into a corner, all she does is start swinging. I couldn't let my husband, my friends or my family know. This was going to be all on me. I was going to get through this or die trying. Thank God this was during cold and flu season, so I could fake an illness to cover.

I told my family to just stay away, I must have the flu! I took off nursing school and prepared to die. I remember never being comfortable. I remember sweating and freezing, sleeping and insomnia, body aches all over, like I've never felt before. My original pain was intensified, and let's not forget the constant vomiting and diarrhea. I remember taking over-the-counter sleep meds just so I could sleep through the process of withdrawal as much as possible. I remember googling my symptoms and other people's withdrawal stories. I was so humbled. I had no idea how many people are going through withdrawal on their own at any given moment across the world. I remembered feeling like I understood them all. I shared my story with a few people but mainly just read and prayed for them and myself. At every moment it seemed I would pray and beg for the next minute to be a little easier than the minute before. It was such a humbling experience to feel your entire body literally screaming at you for the choices you made. Not for minutes or hours, but days and weeks. Even months and years for some of the sensations or thought processes to fade away. I did it all to myself but, we are reminded old habits die hard.

I remember going back to nursing school thinking I would get kicked out if I missed any more days. I was living on an over-the-counter arsenal to treat every withdrawal symptom I had. I paced the back of the classroom many times because it helped ease the discomfort in my body. I am sure that was not weird or noticeable right? I often wonder who really knew me then? I was unapproachable; I would have died to bury that secret. No one would have dared confront me then.

I managed to survive serious withdrawal, by the grace

of God. I struggled with feeling like death, but still hiding it the best I could for months. I was at my maximum of thirty 5mg Percocet tablets a day, or the equivalent, when I forced myself into self-withdrawal. Even as a full-blown addict, I still maintained the extreme independence and workaholic coping skills I had learned as a child. "No one will care about me or love me if they know the truth. My only worth in life is what I can do for others or my personal achievements," is what I would tell myself. Let's get real, personal achievements get you more praise, right? I felt proud of myself because I survived withdrawal without the help of anyone else. I had survived without any of them. I was invincible! I really had it within myself to come through something so hard by myself. But then, I thought, why would I want to do everything by myself all of the time? I felt better, so I was getting more things done! "Look at that! I can have the best of both worlds! Britni you are a Genius!", I thought. If I could find some pills, I would take them, but control them better this time! I told myself I would take no more than three to five pills or doses a day! Though I didn't always have them, when I did, I would limit myself. My mother was one of my biggest enablers of my addiction. She always had pain pills and if I was ever without them, she would give them to me, or I would just take them. After I got myself "under control" I would go to moms, and I would be reminded why I needed to stay away. Mom would offer me pills, I would smile and simply decline her offer. I was so proud of myself for having my addiction under control! It's so hard for me to write about it now. Knowing that was what self-harming, unloving, compassionate, Britni was thinking about herself. It truly is a heartbreaking perception to have of yourself for so long. I created so much tension in my life and for those close to me. Chances are the people I was around didn't know the depths of despair I was in at any given moment. Oh, the trauma I must have created for anyone who crossed my path, even my children, Where they old enough to understand what was going on with me then? They must have thought I was mean, angry, and spiteful. I was, but I promise you, it was only supposed to be directed toward myself. It was always about what I felt were my shortcomings. failures as a mom and nursing student, wife, etc. You name it, I can fail at it! But these pills, helped me suffer a little less while I failed. They were my crutch.

I held onto this lifestyle cycle for a few more years, until my next guilt-filled adventure took place and the inevitable end of my marriage. My mother was pleased to be able to tell me "I told you so!" She predicted on my wedding day that my husband and I would not last. She was excited ten years later about her prophecy coming to light.

While shockingly, that chapter of my life is considered another commandment broken, it's what eventually saved me. Before my next great tale of woe began.

Angel Number 611

This number indicates that it takes courage and patience to become the person you want to become in the future life. In other words, you have to go through pain to become successful. Avoid negative feelings, change a bad habit and with time everything will be ok. Trust the process.

There is no fear in love, but perfect love casts out fear. For fear has to do with punishment, and whoever fears has not been perfected in love. – **1 John 4:18**

Chapter 6

Faith or Fear

There are only two options in life with how you choose to look at everything. Faith or Fear. Sorry to break it to you. That's it. You can choose to have faith in something bigger than you, or you can choose to live in fear. You can believe good things will happen more often if you project good into the world. Faith. Repeat after me: "I am a child of God; He made me and loves me. The lessons I learn in this life are so that I can learn from my mistakes. In turn, I will help other people know the value of His love and grace." It starts with Self-Love. If you struggle with trusting God, like I had before my struggles, you can insert whatever word makes you feel more comfortable. For example, divine;

meaning of, from, or like God. The life source, your maker, being one with the universe, it is all the same. Even if you choose a more spiritual path, there is only one, and the energy is a full collective of an entire whole. I believe messengers are everywhere and come in many forms. God has strategically placed them in all different areas of the world and in all different religions for a reason. Our faith is really invested into a source that truly cares enough to know each one of his children are individuals, each person is going to react differently to each aspect of their life. Multiple ways have been established for you to tap into the purest of unconditional love, whenever you are ready to do so.

All Religions are necessary because all people are not the same. For example, if we talk politics, there is the Republican, Democratic, and Independent Parties, with a few other smaller ones. Not everyone can agree on every aspect of how to live, nor are they supposed to. Rather, we have a set of a few basic "Rules" or Bill of Rights, if you will. The same goes for religion, the 10 Commandments and the 7 deadly sins. Some day-to-day aspects are different, but most of them teach love and acceptance, right? Love thy self and thy neighbor, don't lie, cheat or steal. And do not get angry, kill people or be jealous, is pretty much the basic common concepts, right?

Not ready to jump on the faith bandwagon yet? Whether you're a parent or not, I'm sure it's easy to picture the following words. You go through so much struggle and hard work, no matter how you bring a baby into your family. Whether you conceived naturally; assisted or artificially, to labor and the birthing processes from natural, pain management or cesarean, all are difficult. What about foster parenting or the adoption process? The paperwork, the waiting, the complete uncertainty. What about the expense or the stress of thinking, is the "real" family going to come back and step in? No matter the how, the struggle is the same, but different.

Side Note: There is a phrase I remember from nursing school that was repeated to me over and over by my favorite instructor, Ms. Susan Stauffer. "It's all the same, but different." (There are so many phrases I hold onto that I learned from people over the years. They all make more sense the more I learn). In life there are so many different perspectives, and many different ways of doing things. Things such as not driving the same way as someone born with no arms, right? That is easy enough to imagine! I watched a show where a young kid drove a car with no arms, just his feet! It has the same end result, just a different pathway to get there! Miss Stauffer used the analogy to describe how different body systems could do the same thing for your body like removing waste in a different way. While each system has its own different unique way to filter waste, it is still just removing waste. I found myself using this phrase for everything! There is not always a clear right and wrong path....it is more like the Eastern vs Western hemisphere, there is more of a right side and a wrong side and at least a million different pathways to get to the same check point.

That is why there is so much grey area in the world. Intentions are everything! It's not always the event that is the problem. If I knocked your favorite vase off your table and it shattered into a million pieces, would you be upset? Probably! Would it make it better or worse if my intentions where to purposely knock the vase off the table because I thought it was a hideous vase? Thinking you should be ashamed of yourself for having such an awful piece of art in your home? Worse, right? How about if I immediately apologized and said, "it was a complete accident, how can I fix this or replace it?" This reaction is better, right? It will never fix the broken vase, but my intentions before the event, AND how I respond to your reactions to the event, will control the outcome.

Talking about Faith, what about the faith it takes to bring a child into this world? We put so much effort into either creating a life or giving a better life to that child, but it takes faith to have a child. Being a parent is the most selfless love out there. When brining a child into the world, you want to give your baby ALL THE THINGS you didn't have. You want your child to be happy, would you want your son or daughter to work long hours at a dead-end job, struggling and living paycheck to paycheck? What about continuously doing for others without even taking the time to shower themself? How about not having meaningful conversations with the people you love for fear of rocking the boat? No, of course not! We want our children to have faith and be happy. Do the things they love without guilt, fulfilling their purpose in life and having the ability to give and receive love freely. We want them to have faith that the universe and God wants that for you also. Your actions as a parent will help the process unfold.

You can choose to live a fear-based life, but that grows into paranoia and anxiety. When we don't trust or believe in the "something more", life is more difficult to handle. It can place all life's weight on our own shoulders. Carrying all this weight, you feel you have nothing. No one to turn to who shows you good things are possible or attainable. There are no words of wisdom when we hit a wall. Life will continue to try and knock you down from time to time either way. Bad things happen to good people all the time. It doesn't mean you are destined for failure, or that you'll always get the short end of the stick. Sometimes hard stuff is just hard stuff. Seek the light and flip the script. Don't internalize rejection! Why is it so much easier for people to live in fear? And why am I so much better at jumping to the negative conclusions? I believe we let fear shut us down. We let fear throw up our walls of protection. If we have the walls up, we also shut out love and all the other good stuff life has to offer. Nothing gets inside the walls, and nothing gets out. I knew my walls wouldn't let the deep hurt get to me anymore. I can trust myself to know that I can and will get through this hardship, and things will always work out for the greater good, eventually, because I picked myself up a thousand times before. But what I never thought about, was not setting myself up for the same patterns and the next failure. I wanted to be able to stop in the middle of a hardship, evaluate all the angles, and see how I may approach it differently. I realized I was still that little girl fighting everyone and everything. Maybe I didn't have to go against the grain, every time. It feels like a never-ending learning process. Your walk with the Divine is one of the best things we can do to fuel our spirit. It's been said, God's grace will fill the space, but only if you allow it.

As much as good nutrition and exercise are essential for your body, so is fueling it. Are you fueling your mind? If you are not filling your mind with good things, then the world will fill it with the bad things. Your spirit and heart need peace as well. Are you creating time to slow yourself down and enjoy the moment? Are you making time every day to check in with yourself or practice gratitude? Do you offer yourself peace and a safe place to land?

Fueling my spirit, mind, body, and soul was a struggle for me at first. After everything I had been through, I didn't trust anyone, let alone God. I didn't freely follow Him or believe His word for a long time. I was hardened by the world I was living in. I really didn't know His word, and I wasn't seeking Him to find out either. It was easier for me to speak about faith in crystals, and divine energy than Jesus or God. Getting to the place I am at now in my spiritual journey, I realize that the Bible and crystals are really all the same. Just more tools he puts into place to help us find him. Let's be real, if your life is perfect and happy all the time then chances are you have no need to go searching for Divine intervention. Or you already have it worked out with the big man himself. He is always there for those of us who are lost and need guidance. He will always meet you where you are in hopes you will find your way back to Him. His people help others by sharing their testimonies and miracles. How they overcame their trials and came out with great favor. Real people living those miracles then and now, and those who know His love and grace, hold onto that. They borrow His courage in the midst of their struggles. They praise Him in rough times and in the peace. They know where they would be without His hope, mercy, and sacrifice.

The Covid-19 Pandemic is the perfect example of faith. Did your job or school come to a screeching halt, suddenly throwing you into quarantine with your family? Did you stay on the couch, catching up on Netflix? Did you slow down and enjoy time with your family instead of having to rush around between sports, activities, or social media? Did you invest in yourself by learning a new skill, trade, or find a new outlook on something? Did you wait for the imminent doom, or did you choose to be optimistic, having faith that there is something to gain from this? Did you and your family grow closer together or further apart? Life will pass you by either way, so your outlook and level of faith can help you gain happiness. I think about it this way, almost every famous person, or person who has achieved something great in their lives, usually thanks God, right? Is that a coincidence? Do they all meet weekly and talk about how to achieve great things? Ok, I know I am being funny now! The point is, what is the harm in adding a little faith to alleviate stress and gain happiness? If religion is not your thing, start by asking and praying to your Divine Self. You know best what area of your life you should be working on. Don't just pretend you are, really do the work.

God teaches He will get the Glory; however, actions always speak louder than words. So if you love yourself first, that is a great place to start because He does too! He knows you will see the truth and find Him. Some people cut it close by waiting until they are on their death bed to find Him, but some are disciplined enough to do better because they know better! Strive for progress not perfection. Little changes will always snowball into bigger changes, you choose their trajectory. Chip away at the old, unnecessary walls you have built, so you can find the love that's been waiting for you to accept it. All you need is a little faith.

For me, it has always been a more spiritual practice, but I'm still surrounding myself with God. I would like to think I'm gaining a better understanding of His word these days. It doesn't really matter to me what you call it, the practices and guidelines are close enough and at least on the same hemisphere. It can all be defined by the word Love. As I said earlier, all religions are necessary because all people are not the same. I truly believe the good Lord knew exactly what He was doing when He created all His children to be unique individuals. With our own free will. Each religion has the same basic concept, a set of rules or commandments that guide us to live our lives more loving and God like. Everyone is different, though. We can't even agree on a President, let alone a way to live our everyday lives. So, there are options in life that will ultimately lead you to the same destination. Make sense? What if a Jewish man lives his entire life as a loving, caring husband, and father who gives back to his community often, a pillar of his town, loves the Lord, and shares his wisdom with all those that need it? He's definitely getting into Heaven, right? How about the Christian man who does the same? Does one outshine the other in Gods eyes over a few verses? What if it was the same scenario for someone who is gay? I'm not here to debate religion or lifestyle choices. Which lifestyles are right or which are wrong. I feel all lifestyles have a divine purpose, so go out there and find your people! The kicker is, none of that stuff really matters if you don't truly know Him. The relationship is what He is after, so if you go to church and do Godly things, without the relationship, the grace won't be enough. Find your tribe and love them fiercely. It allows more opportunities for people to know faith and love. Frankly, if you are being critical towards someone else's faith or lifestyle choices, that's not loving your neighbor, nor is it in God's teaching. Hate the sin, love the person, and leave the judgement to the King.

Choose faith and believe, start acting as such. Believe the universe conspires to bring you happiness because it does. So then, why do some people struggle with faith? It is hard to say. For me, I have been conditioned by past hurts, and child-hood traumas. I don't recognize the negative in others in order to protect myself. I don't even realize I still have the defense mechanisms I had built. I've been closed off and dissociated for as long as I can remember. It's easier to act like you don't need help, then to trust someone to show up for you. After all, they can still let you down like all the others. Or is that just me?

Jamilia White, an amazingly inspiring psychic and coach, explains it best in her famous Trauma Response post:

"The inability to accept support from others is a trauma response: Your "I don't need anyone; I'll just do it all myself" conditioning is a survival tactic. You needed it to shield your heart from abuse, neglect, betrayal, and disappointment from those who could not or would not be there for you. Whether it was created by the parent who was absent and abandoned you by choice or the parent who was never home from working three jobs to feed and house you. Or the lovers who offered sexual intimacy but never offered a safe haven that honored your heart. Or the friendships and family who always took more than they ever gave. Or all the situations when someone told you "We're in this together" or "I got you" then abandoned you, leaving you to pick up the pieces when life got real, leaving you to handle your part and their part, too.

So, because of all the lies and all the betrayals, you learned along the way, life taught you, that you just couldn't really trust people, or better yet, that you could trust people, but only up to a certain point, or that you can't trust the choices you make in choosing the people you surround yourself with. Extreme independence is a trust issue. We are programmed to never put ourselves in a situation where we have to rely on someone, "I won't have to be disappointed when they don't show up for me, or when they drop the ball... because they will always drop the ball, eventually right?"

Or even better, you may even have been intentionally taught this as a protection strategy by generations of hurt ancestors who came before you. I personally come from a long line of angry defensive women. Extreme independence is a preemptive strike against heartbreak. So, you don't trust anyone, and you don't trust yourself, either, to choose people, the right people. To trust is to hope, to trust is to be vulnerable and have faith. "Never again," we vow. But no matter how we dress it up and display it proudly to make it seem like this level of independence is what we have always wanted to be, in truth it's your wounded, scarred, broken heart behind a protective brick wall.

You are worthy of having support. You are worthy of having true partnership, worthy of love, and worthy of having your heart held. Worthy to be adored, worthy to be cherished, worthy to have someone say, "You rest. I got this." And actually, deliver on that promise. You don't have to earn it, you don't have to prove it, you don't have to bargain for it, and you certainly don't have to beg for it. You are worthy. Simply because you exist."

Wow was she ever right! This post is what started my search for real deeper healing.

I loved being a powerhouse! I was impenetrable, nothing gets in. Certainly, no hurt gets in, but neither does love. Fortresses and armor are for those in battle, or who believe the battle is coming. It's a trauma response. How hardened have you become because of a few people in the world? Think about that, just for a second. There are over seven and a half billion people in the world. That's a seven, a five, and eight zeros. There are a lot, yet we tend to worry about the opinion and actions of the wrong handful? Why are we afraid to create healthy boundaries with the wrong few? The good news is, trauma that is acknowledged is trauma that can be healed.

Angel Number 711

This number tells us to focus on the opportunity and new projects in your life. You have made wise decisions and choices. You are spiritually evolving. Continue to release old fears and beliefs learned from your childhood or early adulthood, so you can transform into your true self. Live in tune with your heart, your heart will always tell you what you really need, not what you want.

Let the morning bring me word of your unfailing love, for I have put my trust in you. Show me the way I should go, for to you I entrust my life. – **Psalm 143:8**

Chapter 7

The One

This chapter is my favorite! Not just because of the really hard lessons I learned and overcame, or because I finally completely understood life, but because it is the final piece of my healing journey.

I remember the very moment I saw him. I had just started as a nurse at a County Prison. I had been on this new path in life, starting about 6 months prior. Story Time: 6 months prior, I was the heaviest I had ever been. My youngest daughter Phoenix Monroe Harrell, had just Celebrated her 1st birthday. I fought hard to have that little girl, from talking her father into having her, a harder time trying to conceive her and an entire rough pregnancy. I found out she had no amniotic fluid, and then of course a difficult delivery during "Fall Back". She Made her entrance known and still does; she is my little warrior but still as kind and soft as can be...When she wants to be!

But by January of 2016 she had already turned one, and this momma was sick of her life. Fed up! I was overweight, stressed out, and numbing the pain in all the wrong ways. My marriage was also seemingly nonexistent. We worked well together for the greater good of the home, or family, but as far as a couple, I had been sleeping on the couch for over a year. I was depressed and lonely. I needed change. I was embarrassed by how far I let myself go. I was ashamed of the woman I had become and was still using. I had to do something.

I started working out at home which was rough to start, but my reasons for wanting better, pushed me through. I added lifestyle changes to my diet, slowly. I had been a nurse; I knew the yo-yo diet merry-go-round trends and I was determined to do it right this time. Small changes I was willing to maintain, the majority of the time. Cheat days are a thing Y'all! Important in fact! Take your cheat days! I knew consistent small steps create great change, and an explosion in the beginning, will only last as long as you have that energy....it will always run out. Then you are left with more of the same. Energy is needed to do everything, it is like my physics' teacher said, or maybe it was a pain reliever commercial? A body in motion stays in motion. Energy is needed for everything, so you must replenish it. How do you do that? Short answer... by seeking the light.

What you focus on the most, whether in a good light or bad, you will create more of it. Old habits die hard. How determined are you to break them? When life gets the hardest, and you have not restocked the energy you need to continue the change, or have a new way already planned out. The simplest next step, and often what most people, not just us addicts do, is revert back to default programming. Its comfortable, no matter how bad the old habit is, it is always going to be more comfortable than the new. This road is easier because I'm already doing it and have done it, I know what to expect, but I was determined not to be fat!

In 6 months, I had lost 50 pounds doing a couple Beach Body programs. My body and mind shifted some. I was happier with myself as a person, but my life was still not where I wanted it to be. I had calmed down on not wanting to be fat and was ok with healthy. Now I needed happy! Next was my career. My nursing job at the time was sucking the life out of me. That was next on my list. I started applying everywhere. I remembered my husband at the time showing me the ad for the prison nursing job. "Oh, you want me to go to work and get shanked? Thanks Babe!" was my instant reaction. I remember adding it to my list because who couldn't use the interview practice. I had 5 interviews scheduled, and I was excited for something new.

The prison interview was second on my list. I was so nervous about it, but I was very intrigued. I had seen people in my life get arrested a few times, and I had been in to visit some of those people before, but I personally never been on the inside of a jail. It was so funny, that was the first question the interviewer asked. I had been to placement and youth facilities, but not a "real prison". After the interview, I just HAD to accept the position. I had always been an Investigation Discovery addict, and maybe this was my dream job. I took it as a sign and handed in my two weeks' notice.

So, two weeks into my new job at the prison, I was working day shift, but my ultimate goals was third shift. I was there to do a second shift med pass and was leaving for the day. I was turning in my keys when I walked past the Lieutenant's office and peaked in; they always wave. And there he was sitting at his desk. He was bald and clean shaven; in an all-grey uniform I had only seen a handful of people wearing in there. Our eyes met. I had never seen him before, and I promise you I cannot replicate the sound I heard in my head that moment. It sounds crazy to me writing this out, it was a bell or ding almost like a cartoon with the lightbulb, signaling a great idea or finally it all clicks. I heard the voice in my head louder and clearer than I have ever heard it before saying "Follow him, he will be important in your journey". I am pretty sure I awkwardly smiled and went home.

Listen, I know what you are thinking, I am a married woman! Yes, and I had already been down the cheating and being cheated on path, but I promised myself I would do better. I wasn't so sure why I received the message I did, but I was intrigued. What could I learn this time? Little did I know then what God had in store for us all.

Shortly after the first sighting, I realized he was going to be one of my regular Shift Commanders. For privacy purposes in this book, we will call him Lance. Their job is to run the show, and my job is to report need to know information and medical judgment to assist the Shift Commanders in doing their job.

Simple enough. I do that for doctors, right? Oh, I was so wrong!

The first time I stood next to him and shook his hand, I felt his energy. My entire body reacted to this man. And I am not just talking about hormones, to see him in uniform, or that I just hadn't had any in a while. I am talking electric sparks radiating through my entire body, causing a tingle inside me from the tips of my toes and fingers, to the crown of my head. My heart and mind, I swear, must have exploded with how much pressure I felt from the sparks. With no explanation, when our hands touched, I also felt his pain. I had no idea why my body was reacting this way, or what was happening to me. To my relief, I learned he was married, so I won't have to worry about the sparks I had. We could just work together and be great friends. We started sharing stories about our lives and in some ways, we were very similar. In other ways we were on the complete opposite end of the spectrum. It was so weird, but we both quickly realized we were living a very similar home life. We were both dominant but stubborn.

I was on this new path to discovering myself and even started a brand-new business venture on the side. I was now a consultant for Pure Romance, a business where I could make money selling intimacy products! How fun! Pure Romance ended up being a game changer for me and my life. In learning about these products and how they help other women, I learned more and more about self-care, self-love, business, and ways to enhance foreplay and intimacy. I was helping married women stay married, and single women stay safe. Plus, a lot of the women I had helped, had also been through trauma or abuse, I was able to help them get their sexy back, and reignite passion at home. Maybe I could do more of that, giving him advice and tips for his relationship. Let's face it, I have dealt with tons of hard stuff, so his hard stuff was no biggie to me. I could help by offering advice and vice versa. Sounds like I had it all figured out huh? In learning his struggles, I felt it harder to ignore the obvious, but oh-so wrong, "I don't want to go down this road again" feeling. The first time we crossed our boundaries with a kiss. I felt so alive and desired in that moment. I was on cloud nine, but I had to go home, instantly feeling regretful. What was I doing (again)? I had gotten so good at ignoring guys and their cheap comments. They all want the same thing, remember! I have one of the good ones! I tried to beat this into my head over and over again. So I blocked him on all social media and shut it down. I couldn't do this again.

We still saw each other at work though. We had to work together on some level, and he seemed to be everywhere I turned. (Red Flag). I remember how persistent he was. How I thought that he really must've cared about me if he was trying this hard. Every time I stood next to him I could feel my entire body react. Is this what they meant by "The One" and "You will just know?" At home, I tried to get some type of reaction out of my husband. I got nothing back from him. I suppose I knew the marriage had been over for a while, and nothing was ever going to change. I felt overcome with defeat again. I began to pray and meditate often. I needed to know why I was in this situation again. What was His plan? How do you follow and listen to God, when you know you are getting ready to sin? Why would He bring this magnetic man into my life when he can never be mine? God will never send you someone else's husband, right? Why am I even having these conversations with myself when I know the answer I am supposed to give and the path I am supposed to follow? Why am I receiving these confusing messages from above?

I have always had moments when I "just knew" some-thing even if I really didn't. Was it intuition, God's favor, or psychic capabilities? Whatever you call it I didn't know what it was or why it was happening. I learned from previous life choices, that I heard this voice and its messages clearer when I was sober. The clearer my head the clearer my pathway to heaven was, sort of. I was not sober completely though and the messages I received about Lance were so loud and undeniable, but they were not logical, either. What do I trust?

We had sex anyway. (Red Flag) The first night we met was easily the best night of my life at the time, and the worst. I feel like I was living in a split world. Like the Angel and Devil were on my shoulders! Here in front of me was everything I needed and wanted in a man. He was a leader, strong and assertive. He knew how to make choices and run the show like me. People feared him but the most important part was that he was soft with me. I was allowed to see a side of him others were not privileged to see. I had a lot of conversations with myself, about should I, should I not, what will happen to our children, and families, etc. will it be worth it? What if it is a lie and he will never leave his wife and I am alone? In that moment, that voice spoke again. "He deserves to be happy too."

Oh, my goodness, of course! My husband deserves to

have a wife that wants what he wants, but I didn't. There is no way anyone could tell me that man was happy. He was comfortable and used to his routine. He is one of the most selfless men I have ever known, and I knew he would never leave me. He had to have known about a lot of things, but chose to let "me do me". He never required me to do better, and I never willing jumped at the opportunity for him. I was still using drugs regularly, and I began to realize how angry I was. I surrounded myself with people who would never speak up against me or put me in my place. Lord knows, I should have been put in check a long time ago. Regardless of what people thought of me, I did want to be with Lance. It was the first time ever, I made a self-less choice for my husband. I was going to require him to love himself more and find someone better for himself. I knew he would never do that on his own accord. We always make better choices when we are forced to rock bottom right? He deserved better than he had been dealing with too. We had been on this hamster wheel long enough.

I also knew at this point, regardless of what Lance decided to do with his life, I could no longer fake mine. We all deserved better, and someone needed to stand up for us. Why was it always me though? Why do I always have to be the one? "Because you are the one who is strong enough", the voice would say in response. Ok here we go, I always do a 1, 2, 3, Go! Right before a big moment. Somehow it helps.

So, I had the hard conversation with my husband and I asked for a divorce. I chose to not to disclose my infidelity, but I am sure he was aware of it. I didn't want to tell him because I didn't want to add fuel to the fire. I wanted Lance to make his own choice because he wanted to, not because he was forced to. I didn't want him to have me by default. My husband and I went through the hard stuff and told our kids. I found an apartment, which he helped me move into, and I bought him a kayak. Why I did that, I don't really know. Maybe I was trying to make him feel better, or myself. When he filed for divorce, we created a custody schedule. I was not upset or bitter. I was just ready for something different and wanted him to find himself too.

I received confirmation I had made the right choice two weeks later, when the news of my husband's new girlfriend moving with him hit. I felt hurt at first, then I yelled at myself asking WHY it hurt me. Then it hit me, I was hurt because I realized in that moment, we had both chosen to stay somewhere we didn't really want to be, for the sake of our kids. It pains me to realize so many years were wasted because we refused to accept that change is what we both needed in order to grow. My babies adore their new stepmom and siblings. but no family is 100% rainbows and glitter 24/7. I'm just grateful he is happy now. He and his new wife deserve it.

I had my own apartment now, and Lance had a key. He could come and go whenever he pleased. He continued to tell me he wanted our relationship and was willing to find a way to make it happen. I blindly followed along with him.

I confided in Lance the story of my bad addiction days, leaving out that I used to use narcotics. He made it very clear that he would never be with a "criminal" as he used to put it. No one had ever put a boundary on my drug use that I couldn't bend. After all, I had it "under control" anyway. So, what he doesn't know, won't hurt him. If I knew he was serious about me, I would get serious too, but I left it at that and didn't tell him about that part of my drug use.

I was struggling alone in my apartment often, when the kids were at their dads and Lance was home with his family. I thought to myself, this is your karma. You have ruined so may lives and this is your payback. I struggled to trust the miracle of what God is doing in my life knowing what was happening with Lance and I and what we were causing.

We were getting to a point where Lance was going to make a move. He came over to my apartment before I got home so we could spend the day together. When he found my door was open, because of his security background, he went in to check things out. What is the problem with that you ask? It sounds sweet right? It was! However, I forgot to shut my underwear drawer that morning and on display was a bottle of fun for the addiction I had "under control." The addiction I had lied to him about because I wanted to be with him. He knew. My cries and apologies were not enough. He left me on the floor devastated. I did it again. Well, I had already known I was doing it again, I mean I got caught in a lie, again. I saw that look of disappointment again because I had let him down. I loved him so much, and I had promised if he made a move toward a life with me, I would too, but I was not willing to do it just for me. That is a sad realization to admit to now. I flushed most of it in front of him, the rest I used to step down over the next few days. I am no dummy, I have been through detox before. This one would be cake! I had chosen to do it in hopes that he would eventually see the change in me and come back. I was going to do it this time, because of him, but for me. And I did, minus a few hiccups.

He did come back, but to be honest, I think he forgave me more because a few weeks earlier, the situation was reversed. I had found messages on his phone, that he would normally keep under strict lock and key. (More Red Flags!) He had a wife and me but was still messing around with other women. I struggled with letting go of the poison and numbing the pain, and he struggled with seeking attention from other women when he wasn't being validated at home, whether he earned it or not. He made me believe we had both messed up and we should just forgive and do better.

All of this was happening while Lance's father was losing his cancer battle. As if the world wasn't hard enough right? His father passed away and Lance just shut down. He went into auto pilot for two weeks before he finally spoke about it and cried. I am reminded that when life gets hard, you can keep stepping forward, or revert back to old habits. I kept stepping forward. Lance never really had to go through many traumatic events. Not like me at least. His parents were still together, a religious couple, and Lance was brought up with a solid foundation, even though it wasn't a perfect family life. I knew this was going to be difficult for him, but I was a fixer.

He said over and over again that a life with me was what he wanted, and he was ready to move forward in making it a reality. After having our affair for a year and a half, he was ready to tell his wife. Somehow, I feel like she was ready for her out too. Especially since I wasn't the only one he had cheated with during their marriage. (More Flags?).

As we began to merge our lives, I met my "bonus son." He's a kind, caring, and creative boy, who loves to be helpful. He is extremely curious but it often got him into trouble. He is four months younger than Phoenix; so basically, we inherited a set of twins. I don't know how you mommas and daddies of multiples do it, when just one can be rough! I have so much respect for parents of multiples, and I'm grateful I didn't have to do this during the infant stage. Celebrate the little victories.

Our first year together was easy. We were separating old lives, creating a new one and we just worked well together. We fought some, but it was rare. When we did fight, it got heated fast. The smallest fights turned into huge blow ups. (We loved the color red!) I wasn't always sure why they got so heated, but we always talked it out. Plus, who doesn't love some amazing make up sex?

I was there for him when he was struggling and vice versa. I put time and effort into the care I provided in the home and so did he. We had this connection and attraction, and it was just magic. We traveled often and made time for each other with weekly date nights or monthly adventures. Some with the kids and some just us. Not to long before we got engaged his old habits resurfaced. He had sent a private message to another girl we both knew. Of course she sent me the screen shot. He denied it and I posted it. That's right, public Facebook Post! I was calling him out on his bull shit. Not long after posting it, I received messages from women who shared similar experiences (Apparently, I love all the flags). Some of the women were married, some were single, looking for "the one". One of the married women even met Lance at Sheetz to "catch up." I was devastated to say the least. I felt like it was karma. It brought me right back to a place I knew oh so well. All the bad that I had done was being corrected now. After a huge blow up, I asked his mother to step in. The bible says to seek counsel if you have trouble in your marriage. I reached out to his mom because she knew him better than anyone else. Someone needed to talk him off a ledge because he was threating the women who were telling me their side of the story! He eventually spoke some truth about it and took ownership of his wrongdoings. Later, I found out he gave me those little tidbits of "truth" because with one of the girls I was I was speaking to, he was forceful and didn't want me digging further. All of this was beyond my comprehension, and I felt like I had been sleeping with the enemy.

I was not ok though. I didn't understand why I wasn't enough for Lance. I was better at household chores, I learned to cook better, I was trying to be the definition of superwoman. In secret, I was also still using occasionally, but this time it really WAS occasionally. I was sober more days than not but still not 100%. How could I keep calling him out for his crap if I was still struggling with mine? (More manipulation and control tactics) I didn't trust him though; I knew there would be more eventually. So, I waited and watched. I can recognize now that proposing to me is how he got me to stay this time. There was always a gift or some big trip to right his wrongs and help me forget. Man, I did get a lot of things and trips during our short relationship.

Not too long after this, my shadows came to the light, again. This time a longtime friend caught me stealing her stash. She called me out on it, and I instantly apologized greatly. I was sober most days, so I knew I didn't truly need it, but why were my habits of how I got it still a "thing?" I promised I would never give her reason to question me again, because her friendship was way more important than any drug so I decided to get real with the last part of my drug habit! I begged her for forgiveness, and I stayed true to my word, I was done. I never stole anything ever again. The only time I had narcotics was during a dental procedure, which were prescribed by a doctor. I never told Lance about the incident with our friends. I never brought it up, or openly admitted to it.

About a year later, in casual conversation, it had come up between our husbands that I had stolen drugs. To be honest, I had forgotten about it. I obviously did not want Lance to know at the time, plus. I had gotten it together and had been sober since then. I let it go, but he never got the opportunity to. As you can imagine that did not go over very well with him. I reminded him of his recent indiscretions, and we left it at that. That made three for three chances we both blew at getting it right.

Angel Number 811

According to this angel number, you are capable. You can build your own life. You can create your own luck and change your destiny. 811 is also inspiring you to love the work process, not the result. To love the journey, not the destination. Abundance is coming.

When you pass through the waters, I will be with you: when you walk through fire you shall not be burned, and the flame shall not consume you. – **Isaiah 43:2**

Chapter 8

Happily, Ever After

Remember the woman I call mom? The one who is strong and independent and can handle anything, but also got her way through intimidation, control, manipulation, and being the loudest one in the situation. Women like her win by default because they don't give up and giving in is not an option. Oh yea, and they have anger issues! This is the type of woman that I called home for a long time in my life. I learned a lot of my coping and relationship skills from her. I really thought I had calmed down a lot with my previous marriage but I was so confused why Lance was able to get such a reaction out of me now. No matter how much I thought I was doing better with my anger, I really wasn't. I had subconsciously placed myself into situations where I wouldn't have to react because I was never going to be required to. I avoided any and all triggers, or possible triggers so it wouldn't be a problem. Lance continued to drift away from the man I met and fell in love with which was very confusing to me. He seemed to use my triggers against me. I thought I was being more open and honest with my husband to aid in my healing, but in reality, I was just handing him all the ammunition he would ever need to hurt and manipulate me.

Every time I reacted like a crazy person towards Lance, I was then apologizing for the escalation I caused but never the issues or behaviors that caused the fight. It didn't hit me till much later what was really happening here. Or why, in his mind, my being a drug addict somehow justified his multiple secret encounters with other women online or in person? I was still "In the life."

I continued to work hard and fight for the life I thought we wanted together. Lance needed to get out of his job in corrections, he was becoming more negative, angry, and paranoid the longer he stayed. The type of mindset needed to run a place like that takes a toll on you after a while. You start to imagine everyone you meet out in public is just like the "bad" people you meet in jail. He was hardening more and becoming angrier. He also struggled with anxiety and depression. He was taking medications for it, (when he remembered to take them). The mental aspect was just too much, and the fear of the unknown at times just paralyzed him. He talked about leaving the job but wouldn't actually take any steps to create the change. Luckily for me, the prison appointed a new warden, and she seemed to want to give Lance the boot, along with the majority of the rest of the prison employees too. It was going to come to an end one way or another. He ended up leaving the prison job, took a pay cut, and went to what I refer to as a jail for kids. He figured it would be less work, less pressure, and he could take a breather. Maybe reconsider what he wanted to be when he grew up. In the end, he was fighting more with the kids than he had with the adults. The new job wasn't any better, he needed to try again.

Financially, I was killing it with Pure Romance. I won free trips and bonuses from them plus I had a cake nursing job. I strategically placed myself in nursing situations where I would no longer be around any narcotics. Out of sight out of mind. I was doing in-home care for pediatric patients. Kids are so resilient; and they rarely ever get narcotics at home. I had a steady schedule with the sweetest little boy. He needed nursing care because he was on a ventilator at night. His parents were just as amazing. The mom was easily my best friend at the time, and I loved being able to help her out.

Lance decided he was going to leave the corrections jobs and try his luck at sales again. He had done it in his younger years and liked it then. I was excited for him and knew he was a smooth talker. The prison life was making him bad to people. He handed in his notice and got everything he would need to start on this new business venture: new clothes, new shoes, and an iPad. He was excited, and I was excited for him plus, I was ready for "My Lance" to finally come back! A few days before he was getting ready to start, the world shut down. Covid 19 had caused mass shutdowns and forced unessential businesses to close. His sales job was gone. He ended up having to withdraw his notice at "kid jail" and stayed put. I feared he would never jump again. To my surprise, he was handed another opportunity rather quickly. I remember laughing when he told me he was going to sell roofs! "Aren't you afraid of heights?" I asked! He agreed and laughed as well. I would always rock the Ferris wheel or ski lifts just to hear him freak out! He didn't think I was funny. Lance quickly excelled at his new roofing gig. He was killing it, even earning a company truck. I was so proud of him. A little while later, it was pointed out that he only used a mostly girl crew. Somehow it didn't surprise me much. He loves his women.

It was my turn for change next. I was no longer in love with nursing. In fact, the only reason I was still doing it was for the little guy's momma. She needed consistent help, and I was the only consistent night shift nurse in her area. The Pandemic caused a huge shift in the medical community that I no longer wanted to be a part of. I also wanted a normal sleep schedule, I was over the 3rd shift life. I wanted to find something I could do alongside Pure Romance. I knew so many different women from my Pure Romance business, so what other service could I provide? Ask and you shall receive, right? A girlfriend I met through my Pure Romance business randomly reached out and asked if I ever thought about doing Real Estate? Well, that actually sounds like an awesome idea! I wonder if I could do it?

Lance was making enough money at this point; he could handle the bills by himself for a hot minute, while I started classes. I decided to wait until after our wedding to start real estate classes. We got married on July 11, 2021, on the beautiful beaches of Siesta Key Florida. We could no longer keep our regular destination wedding on the Beaches of Grenada during the shutdown, but Florida stayed open. It was truly the best day ever, just us with a couple of friends. The ceremony was perfect, and I was very impressed by his vows too! It was everything I had always dreamed of. I felt so in love, and excited to build a life with this man, doing it "right" this time! We came home from our wedding and had one of the best receptions I have ever been to in my life! I may be biased, of course, but it was so much fun! Our reception included a slip n slide for the kids and adults, ending with a huge firework display (which we received a fine for later). If you know, you know!

After the wedding, I got down to business and started the Real Estate Program in August. I struggled with all the new terminology and had really thought I was smart. I was a nurse for years and I could do that job in my sleep. I can literally save your life! But I realized quickly that I really knew nothing in this area. I was starting from scratch. But I was determined to finish the program and start work as soon as I could. I already had a job; it was just a matter of getting the license. Covid slowed the process down but, I finished my classes in 3 months versus the given 6 months and waited 12 weeks to get my license from the Real Estate Commission, after I passed my boards. By January 11, 2021, I was working as a Real Estate Agent in full swing. I was already great with people and learned the paperwork process quickly. I closed my first two transactions in March, with no sign of slowing down. I had a lot of transactions where I had to ask my Mentor "Is this normal?" They definitely were not. I ended up doing quite a few difficult deals my first year, even to the point I had certain lenders tell me I should be going after easier jobs! I'm so sorry, I promise I don't intentionally go looking for trouble. I mean I don't want to be doing difficult deals either, no one does. We all want to sign on the first house at the first meeting and not have to bug them till closing day. It's just not how it works, and if I know there is a way to get it done, why would I not disclose that?

Either way, I finished out my first year with 13 transactions and a sales volume of $2,584,000. I was so proud of myself. Plus, Lance had an amazing year too, so we celebrated by taking the kids to Gatlinburg, TN for Christmas! One of the new family traditions we started was Santa bringing a trip to our house, instead of gifts. We went down right after Christmas, staying through New Year's Day, in a super cute cabin with an amazing view! It really is one of our favorite places and I'm so grateful we got to share that with our babies. I never stopped working though, I had a closing on a house while I was in TN, and I came home to some craziness I had to sort through. But I love it, and I mean it. I have never dealt with more crap at times, but I also have not loved a career so much. I finally found my calling and I am good at it! Shortly after getting back into the swing of things at home, my world shifted again.

I had caught Lance messaging women again (My final flag). Devastated was an understatement, but I was not surprised at all. I completely lost my shit. I jumped right back into old habits, and I reacted. I hit him for the very first time, threw things, broke things, and yelled. I became the person I had fought so hard not to be. I needed to leave. I stayed at a cheap hotel, not knowing how long I would really be there. Lance was mad at my reaction, and so was I! However, I was not going to get over his actions anymore, nor did I want this marriage or any parts of him. I'd had other suspicions about missing money, plus his attitude just sucked. I was realizing he was not the man I fell in love with. I hadn't seen that guy in a very long time. I wondered, again, why I wasn't enough? Why was he still searching for whatever external validation elsewhere? I cried on the floor of the hotel, begging God for direction. I didn't care if I had him or had to walk away from him. At this point in my life, I just wanted peace and love. If Lance was incapable of delivering that, then I was cool with moving forward alone. I then remembered every hotel room has a bible. I hear you! In case you have not learned by now, I am big into repeating numbers and their messages, I see them often. I was staying in room 211, so that is the page I opened the Bible to and started reading first. On page 211, there is also chapter 11.....ok I'm really listening. Leviticus Chapter 11 is basically speaking about obedience for God's people, in what they were allowed and not allowed to eat. I really didn't understand at that moment, what this was supposed to mean. I read a few other sections looking for peace and received my validation in other verses that night. I was determined to never let anyone cause me to react that way again, I don't care who you are or what you do, I needed to control myself and present myself in the manner I wish to be treated. What's really funny is the next Sunday, Elevation Church released a new sermon on YouTube called "When Never Meets Now" and Pastor Steven Furtik talks about Leviticus 11 and how it is not about the diet. Wow! I was just blown away; He went on to say it is about your faith and your frame of reference, as well as the discipline it takes to truly follow the Lord's guidance and word. It was an amazing message, handpicked for me. Up until now, I had always pictured Lance as my gift from God, I had changed and grown so much because of my relationship with him. The Lord put him in my life, to hold me accountable for my actions. Just like the Pastor said in his sermon, "Maybe God sent him to my life to help polish me and continue on God's project, which is me." He went on to say, "When people annoy you, they become sandpaper." I had come so far but still had some work to do. I was still processing the fact that this healing process Lance and I were on had been one-sided, when in reality Lance was really doing everything in his power to pull me back in and keep me under his spell.

I remember the moment I realized Lance and I did a lot of things right, but we were still in a very toxic and controlling relationship. He had perfected manipulation at this point, so he told me that my past trauma history was a big part of our disconnect. I had been going to therapy for months at this point, hoping he would join me, so we could both understand each other's mess and how to fix it, if we can. He started going to individual therapy with the same therapist I had, and promise to start couples therapy soon, so I watched but still made plans to leave in quiet.

Angel Number 911

This Angel number indicates angels are close to you and are here to help you achieve your goals. 911 shows up when you are afraid about moving forward. This number showers you in courage to pursue your life goals. Your Angels hear you and are here to help guide you.

In the same way, husbands ought to love their wives as their own bodies. He who loves his wife loves himself. -**Ephesians 5:28**

Chapter 9

Déjà vu

I knew this place well. Rock bottom and I meet again. This time it was deeper. I had been sober for a few years, I was in therapy, and I was learning how to process my emotions and what they each were supposed to feel like. I was unlearning my childhood trauma responses, and now I was knocked back down by my husband, the one who promised me so many times that I was "the one" and he would stop with other women. The one who promised me we would be different. I felt absolute defeat. I spent our entire relationship trying my best to get it right but I was never going to be able to control someone else's feelings or reactions towards me. Whether I did everything right not, my love alone has never and wasn't ever going to be enough. It wasn't enough for my mother and father; it wasn't enough for all of my failed relationships and friendships; it will not be enough for Lance either.

I learned and studied, in Pure Romance, a lot of relationship advice and techniques to reignite the spark in a relationship. Lance was just so angry most of the time, constantly looking for a fight instead of solutions, so I bought him multiple different supplements to try because he kept telling me "IT" didn't work. He literally cried to my face, and said it was his anxiety medication causing the dysfunction, when in reality he was playing the same old game he played with me, his last wife and all the new ladies. The more I tried, the more he pushed me away, giving "them" more attention. I get it, I was once considered part of "them" as well. This seemingly happy successful man was telling me all the right things. How horrible his wife is because she doesn't do XYZ, she nags, she complains, it's toxic, there is no communication, she NEVER has sex with me anymore. Yes, I know, he said it all to me too, and I believed him then. Now the problem was, I was literally doing the opposite. I begged for the attention and intimacy he so freely gave to women who were more broken, and who would believe his lies. Though his ex-wife's main fault was that she didn't make any money. She was a stay-at-home mom who lived off only his paycheck. He clearly couldn't say that about me, his complaints to others about me were that I abuse him. He had a logical reason too, he knew all my trauma, my responses, everything about me, so he played the abuse cycle card. I mean I did hit him, when I was finally done with him in the aftermath of catching him cheating for the millionth time. But just like that song in *Encanto*, "We Don't Talk About Bruno", accountability has never been his strong suit.

I know, quite the sad, woe is me story I played on repeat. I was broken and lost. I struggled to pull myself out of this funk, and just be the woman I wanted to be. I had spent so much time trying to figure out how to get Lance to love me, and keep loving me, I had the right intentions, but clearly the wrong person. My history in life and relationships kept me anxiously attached, but I had no idea I was doing that. People who are anxiously attached generally have low self-esteem and a strong fear of rejection, so we tend to be overly clingy. I have anger issues, so that means I'm the complete package.

In healing my own anger, Lance's anger was clearly revealed, but he never acknowledged his own. His favorite thing to fight with me about was that I was stepping in when he was correcting the kids. He would get so angry and scream at them, belittling them, until I would have enough of it! I talk back some, Y'all. No one stood up for me when I was that kid, I'll be damned if my children get treated that way. We lived separate lives and he rarely had the kids alone. He never saw the abuse he dished out, just everyone's "reactions". In healing my trauma responses, I have learned I married a better version of my mother. I again have been playing the fight vs fawn this entire relationship. It was better in the sense that he didn't physically hit me, but worst in the fact that my mom was stuck with me, Lance chose me I think, because he recognized the damaged moldable woman I was, desperate for a leader.

Therapy has helped me to recognize that I needed to focus on keeping my side of the street clean first. That means holding myself accountable and being responsible for the choices I make. The actions I take to change my negative behaviors and patterns, as well as being in a position to receive the emotion and love around me. Essentially, we must be present and active in our own healing. I like to refer to this as removing your "Hater Vision." If I am easily triggered by something, chances are I'm living in defense mode, waiting for someone to question me so I can defend, be on guard and ready for battle. If we start communicating, there will be a point where I can insert a fight because they are sure to trigger me, and I am ready. I'm sure at one point or another every person gets to this level, but we were living it every other day at this point. That doesn't exactly sound like something you want to run home to, right? I was walking on eggshells every day. Nothing I did could make it stop, he was determined to fight with me. If we fought, he had more time for his women and he could keep hiding money to spend on them. I mean if you are really killing it at something, you would have the statements to prove that right? He hid everything. Tax time was fun y'all! That was an easy choice for him though, he is more concerned with how he looks to the outside world rather than who he really is and truly being authentic.

I knew I just needed to walk and cut my losses, but how? Everything was in his name, and I had no real credit and a history of bad debt. He had control of all of our money, he even took my paychecks for the bills. Plus, he had everyone believing I'm a crazy loose cannon that is just so messed up from her childhood she can't act right. I played right into his game, again.

I prayed and cried and prayed lots more over this question for weeks, not truly knowing what was going to happen or what I was going to do now, alone again with 4 children. I loved him so much and this life we were creating is where I wanted to be, yet I knew he would never stop, and I was the only one fighting for us. I had thought this was real, but it had all been a game to him. I needed and didn't have a willing participant in my partner. I knew I was never going to save this marriage alone, I was never going to make someone love me by the things I did, even though that is the way I was trained to earn love as a child. This realization came to me in the worst way.

My best friend Barbie was losing her cancer battle so my girlfriend and I jumped in the car and road-tripped to Florida to see her beautiful face one more time. She was in the middle of her life when she should be enjoying her life as a new grandma and living it up. Instead, she was transitioning to hospice care at the age of 44. Someday I may not be able to do all the things I want to, and that is not going to be the best time for me to find out my husband is not my person, right? So, I needed to start living for myself first. If Lance was going to leave, cheat or run away and join the circus, then that is what he was going to do. Driving myself crazy to show my worth so he will see it and choose me is super exhausting….. and not worth it anymore. Listen, I am a lover, and my love language is acts of service first, so doing for others is naturally how I show love first, my auto-pilot response. So, waiting on my kids or husband is naturally something I do. I never learned how to say, "I am sorry honey I can't handle that task for you this time because I have (XYZ) happening." They all know how much I do regularly, so they should be able to handle a rejection every now and then. It was my fear that if I didn't do everything when they asked, they wouldn't love me and bounce, but Lance had already dipped out more times than I can count. So what am I fighting to save? What value is he really bringing to my life at this point? None. I knew no matter what, my children and I deserved better.

I made a stand! I was in a place where I wanted healing and to restart, build a new foundation, this time, the right way. Lance was still deflecting and defending himself. He was trying to fight with me, and I decided not to participate in it. I stopped arguing back, I stopped responding. I went emotionless, the grey rock method. I'm pretty sure I scared the man since he was only ever used to my fight and fawn responses with him. I was so exhausted from fighting him and pretty much everyone and everything else in my life. I was just exhausted mentally and physically from life with him. He was just so draining. I just stopped talking and started packing.

He is the type of guy I selected; often intimidating, vindictive, and stubborn. I guess it felt like home. I finally realized the extremely unhealthy dynamic I kept trying to make work. When I finally stopped fighting for us, that's when it all fell apart.

I had practiced forgiveness often before, but only forgiving them as long as they stayed away, or at least they were not ever as close to me as they once were. I would never disrespect them; however, I would never have to deal with or worry about their past or future betrayals again. Once was enough! I had never truly forgiven someone that hurt me and kept them in my inner circle. They would always be moved back further, like on a target. The bullseye is my inner circle and one betrayal, no matter how big or small, would at least get you pushed back a rung. Lance is the only one I had forgiven and still stayed. He hadn't been the closest rung in a long time. I had always kept him back. Protecting more and more of myself from him in fear he would hurt me again. I was just assuming there will be something else I'm going to have to forgive him for. I was just waiting and wondering when I'll find out the next hurtful thing he's done. The funny thing about forgiveness is the more times you forgive for the same thing, the more you realize they never meant the apology in the first place. I didn't know how to truly forgive someone and create a healthy boundary that I could stick to. I didn't exactly know how to do that at first. I removed the fear of being alone and trusted that God was leading me on this path for a reason.

Lance finally agreed to couples therapy, but I guess it was another attempt to get me to stay and forgive, but he stopped showing up after only 3 sessions. I continued individual therapy, Lance was going to individual therapy as well, to the same therapist I was, but kept canceling couple's therapy. I thought we both loved growth and striving for goals. So, it's only natural to be just as committed to growing our marriage as we do a business, a family, or just ourselves right? I'm sure you heard it all before, marriage takes work. Hard, uncomfortable work sometimes. But when you actually do the work, (not just think about it, talk about it, or just plan it out, but taking real action steps to do your part), the results are what everyone wants their marriage to be. This is also one of those things that is much easier said than done. Especially when you are trying to determine what a marriage should look like with an ego-driven, hardheaded, stubborn individual, who is hyper focused on getting a million dollars, topped off with narcissistic tendencies. It's just never going to work. Both people have to be on the same page, at the same time for good results in couples' therapy. In the last couples therapy session Lance and I attended together, I finally felt that I was heard and validated. But when we got home, he screamed at me because he was "blindsided and embarrassed". More proof he had no idea who I really am, what I needed or what I wanted. It was all about him and what other people thought about him.

I couldn't believe what I had gotten myself into, but I do know if you and your partner put in the work to figure it out together you have a good chance of making it. Your partner has seen you at your lowest, and even though they may be upset because you have messed up again, they will love you anyway and will help you back up, and vice versa. You have someone that will keep you in check when you go off course because you know if you mess up again, they may not be as gracious the next time around. You never want them to have to wonder again if they matter. You have someone that you want to do better for and grow with, not because you have to, but because together the two of you are so much better on the good days, and you know exactly where you want to be on the bad ones. When you really think about life without them, it seems unbearable. The type of love that forces you to grow and evolve to a higher version of yourself. Help you grow because you have to be authentic with yourself in order to receive this type of love. Grow with someone that, no matter what, recognizes the hurt in you and does everything in their power to make it right, rather than trying to justify their actions. I did that, I healed myself and now I realize I am worth so much more than this.

He was right about one thing; I didn't know how to regulate my emotions or trust my intuition if severely triggered. Instead of learning how not to be explosive, I just avoided the things, places, or people where triggers were naturally occurring. I rarely faced them, I just avoided all of it, every chance I could get. If a problem started, I just kept my mouth shut and left. I went from being aggressive to being passive, I was an explosive door mat. I had to evolve past this too. I had also placed myself with people that had similar issues. I always found the chaos. Have you ever fought with someone that no matter what is said or done, it gets twisted and manipulated to fit their game plan? It's literally a never-ending battle and usually leaves you questioning everything. Manipulation is real y'all. I can do and say all the right things but if the person receiving the message isn't looking for healing, they will create chaos to avoid it. The narcissist and the empath. I quickly recognized this pattern with a lot of my previous friendships too. Mind Blown. It was the same game I played in my deep addiction days, I knew Lance was in too deep and I needed to get far away.

I was not a door mat, but I also was not the aggressive hot-tempered woman I had become again with Lance`. I was searching for the confident, assertive, kind, and gracious woman I wanted to be. I wanted to trust my own intuition; I was a good person who was no longer willing to allow anyone in my life that made me feel less than who I really am. A child of God, literally doing everything in her power to unlearn living in fear. Especially of the people in her life that are supposed to love her and grow in this new walk of faith. There is a post, I'm not sure where it originated, but I know I have shared it before, and it states, "Don't let Family destroy your family. I don't care who you are. We were raised that family is family and you have to deal with them because they are family. But we were also raised not to talk about trauma and just pray the pain away. Yea, No! The family I am building will be breaking Generational curses. If you disturb my peace, you are no longer welcome in my space. You cannot continue to allow people to cause you emotional harm and keep them around by saying "That is just how they are." No thanks! If they don't want to grow let them go!"

I just love that, and even though letting go can be just as hard as holding on, you can only ever lead someone so far. Their destination depends on how much energy and effort they will put in to changing the situation or fixing the problem with you. Some people are just not capable of change and growth, unfortunately. Or they don't really want to do what it takes to truly achieve it, not just fake it. You don't have to hold yourself back so they can stay in your life. You grow darling, they will catch up or they won't. You must live to your full potential anyway, and never let someone else's actions or reactions hold you back. The world needs you and your purpose.

I have seen more of the world in the short span of my relationship with Lance than I have in my entire life. I take better care of myself now than I ever have, because of Lance. I'm a much better mother, businesswoman, and wife than I have ever been, because of the growth and hurt I've had to endure at Lance's hand. I am a better woman for it now, I fought hard for my marriage even though I didn't truly want to after the 1st time. I fought anyway because what I'd never done before is sought counsel and stayed. It is always easier to lift a couch with two people instead of one. I ran from relationship to relationship because I desperately wanted the full family unit I never had, but I never took the time to actually figure out what I really wanted first. My babies are my family, and I have met so many amazing friends that are easily family now. I didn't need to hold onto the few people who were drilling holes in my lifeboat, no matter what their title in my life was.

I was letting go of my expectations and trusting that God had put me here for a reason. I wanted to actually be able to say we are choosing to stay even though we have more than enough reasons to walk away from each other. It is much like sobriety; choosing to stay clean and fight the good fight, even though it is so much easier to give in and give up. I didn't want that to be the norm here, I wanted to put in the hard work and effort to make Lance and I something incredible and unstoppable. He told me he wanted that too, but dated a few more girls on the side instead. B. Vigil said it best, "The hopeless romantic in me almost cost me, my souls, more times than I can count. My heart has always had trouble accepting what my head already knew."

Angel Number 1011

Angel Number 1011 is communication from your angels, and it would be more helpful if you pay more attention to your intuition, thoughts, and energy. Personal Growth is necessary.

Do not conform to the patterns of this world but be transformed by the renewing of your mind. Then you will be able to test and approve what God's will is – in his good, pleasing, and perfect will.

Romans 12:2

Chapter 10

A Different

Perspective....

I remember when I finally started figuring out the real pieces of my own mind. I started separating myself from my traumas. I began not only recognizing my trauma responses, but I learned why I developed them in the first place. How I can do better, to live as the healed and loved woman that I truly am.

I spent time in my mess, figuring out what my measurement of success was. It's how people feel or what they think about me. I want to be liked. I want people to like me for me, without strings attached. The funny, caring, and gracious woman I wanted to be. The problem is my past, my trauma responses, and the people I chose to love me were keeping me from believing I already had it. I'd been programmed with negativity by the one person who was supposed to show me the light, so I subconsciously chose people that mimicked a better version of that original treatment. It was still comfortable, though. It's what I knew. I never corrected or adjusted my internal defense mechanisms or thought processes. Frankly up until recently, I never even knew they were broken.

I was leaving my power in the hands of the people around me. Let's be real, I wasn't placing myself in the best circumstances or around people that would encourage me to grow and evolve for a large portion of my life. Or people that I could trust with my heart and loyalty. I also rarely made a real choice. I lived in the grey area or middle ground of everything because choosing a side of anything means someone will not like me or agree with me. I had to realize that my choices don't make people like or not like me, it is my reaction or response to their choice that matters. Plus, not everyone is going to like me anyway, it is an impossible goal. Let me tell you, narcissists love when you live in the grey area of life, that is where they prey. If you don't make your own choices and just go with the flow, a narcissist can mold that. What I also realized is I didn't even know what I wanted because I had spent so much time staying in the middle that I rarely acknowledged my own preferences for anything. I struggled with how I got here, and what I needed to do to get back to the real me. I was no longer pretending that my husband didn't have control over me. After all, our relationship started as toxic, and was now even worse. Cindy Cherie's quote hit me hard. "When all you know is fight or flight, red flags and butterflies all feel the same." Wow, that explains the reaction I felt when I met him. Mind Blown.

In studying the different types of trauma responses, I quickly realized I had done them all. There are four regularly recognized trauma responses, fight, flight, freeze, and fawn. (Also known as the 4 Fs of trauma.) Some studies break the last one down into 2 more, it is just whatever helps you best. I can easily see the different levels of reactions for each response and though I had improved overall with the level of intensity in my reactions, I still maintained my trauma responses and therefore a reaction, which could still be escalated. The brain is an amazing mechanism of habit. It had learned to protect me from the danger I had lived in for so long. I was responding to things as if I was still in the middle of that battle again. My responses were valid because I felt fear, however, my responses were inappropriate because I never healed my original wounds. I was on to something.

A fight response would look more like physical fights, yelling, aggression, throwing things, and/or property destruction. When there is a fear (not living in faith) about a certain situation or event, our automatic response system jumps in. Previous similar life situations play a huge part in this. If you are actually being attacked this is a good thing, it will help you survive and fight back! It's the reason a mother can lift a car in a desperate moment to free her child. If you are just having a basic disagreement, not so much. If you have had to actually fight back at least once, that response is already embedded into your subconscious. So, the next time anything big or small triggers that fight response, you are more likely to fall back into that reaction of when you were in that real danger moment. This can be a huge problem when it's something small, such as spilling a glass of juice, or being upset that your husband didn't do the dishes as he said he would. Overreacting or causing a grand gesture because we have been triggered, is never ok. It's good to also note that anger causes the heart to race, and when your heart races your short-term memory shuts off. That is why you think of better things to say after an argument is over, instead of in the heat of the moment. Understanding your trauma and your responses can help you better manage your own behavior. That is all you can control anyway, your OWN behavior, until you can control that, you will never fully see every flower or snake in your own garden.

A flight response includes more avoidant behavior. The flight mechanism is a way to escape the danger, avoid conflict, and isolate ourselves from those around us. Either you just leave the conflict by running away or you "get busy" so there is no time to face the situation. If there was something occurring such as a natural disaster or immediate physical danger, running away is perfect! If it tends to be more of a disagreement and you just leave because you are not winning the argument, you should probably spend some time with yourself and investigate that. All you need to ask for is space when the moment gets intense. In my case, I try to recognize in those moments that I need to take a break, do some deep breathing, and really think about what happened. Why does my body want to respond this way? Before, it would look more like leaving and ignoring that person. Sometimes it was days, weeks, months, even years. I am really good at walling people out and acting as if I don't need or want them around. I've had to do that with my own mother, so anyone else is cake. In reality, I hated it. I want to be liked, but I didn't know I was broken, so I thought that was strength. I was so strong because I wouldn't allow them to hurt me! Unfortunately, it also shows my weakness. I was incapable of having a real conversation about real issues and was again relying only on my feelings. That is not to be confused with removing yourself from a toxic situation or person, those are two different subjects. If you have expressed and attempted to create boundaries with anyone in your life, a parent, spouse, family, or friend, and nothing changes, it's time to bounce. No more, no less.

The Freeze response is very helpful if you use it to slow down and think about what is happening so you can respond accordingly. As a trauma response, it looks more like being frozen like a deer caught in headlights. It looks like dissociating, spacing out, or going emotionally and physically numb or sleeping it off for days or months. Basically, checking out and never coming back to reality; you just stop. I've been good at dissociating also (killing it at life here)! This response can also be helpful when you just need to exit stage left away from a toxic situation, freeze the relationship, and don't look back or engage any longer.

Lastly, the Fawn response is all about people-pleasing. Fawners focus on prioritizing the needs of those around them. For example, if you do everything in your power to diffuse the situation, no matter your feelings about it, for the greater good of the relationship, you are a fawner. You can also be over the top with your energy, or text in all emojis so there is less of a chance to upset someone. (I definitely do that!) This response leaves you feeling unseen, unheard, exhausted, and this just continues the cycle.

With all these trauma responses, some healthy coping skills could look like a relaxation technique (deep breathing techniques, reading a book, prayer, meditation, or taking a nap), physical activity, (going for a walk, maybe some Yoga, or just going outside to get some sunshine) or seeking social support (Calling a friend, seek a support group, church, therapy, or just talk about it).

These trauma responses don't just apply to those of us who have dealt with serious life events. For others, there is something called microtraumas. These are smaller events that can create the same traumatic feeling as a huge event. If you live your life with a bunch of microtraumas and they can add up to something bigger. A stack of microtraumas can create any of the 4 F's in your life. Examples of microtraumas would be, break-ups/divorces, court battles, arguments with your kids and spouses, work-related conflicts, getting fired, or illnesses. Pretty much any crappy event that accumulates over time and compromises a person's self-worth. Perfect, because we don't have enough to worry about! Not only do I have my regular trauma responses working against me, but I now I have my microtraumas too, and my responses were not the healthiest to begin with.

Looking back on my entire life I can pinpoint moments where I have used all of these defense mechanisms when it came to dealing with my mother. I had fought back in my teenage years, then in a desperate attempt to keep my mother in my life and make her happy, I bounced between the flight and the fawn responses. When all else failed, I would practice the freeze for a few days and even tried this for a few years in hopes my mother would finally see the error of her ways and just love me. As life went on, I can easily see these responses in my failed relationships with my children and with Lance. It was easier to break the cycles with my children. I knew they had only known what I taught them, so learning to approach things differently with them would get different responses as well. Lance had to take the time to realize he too had some microtraumas in his life that led to a lot of the major trauma responses without even realizing it or acknowledging it. And unfortunately, just telling someone they have trauma responses and should work on that, doesn't instantly fix the damage that has been done. He had to want to put in the time and effort to figure it out. I wanted to stay and not just for the pretty parts, he was not interested in fixing us. When he ran out of things to blame me for, it simply became "You don't listen."

In writing and editing this book, I realized I had literally changed every toxic trait I had, one at a time in a desperate attempt to get this man to love me, somehow always falling short. Not the best feeling in the world for sure. It was always my fault, and I am just crazy. It was never about his actions, just my responses. When an abuser can no longer control you, they will try to control what other people think of you. The good news? Actions always speak louder than words.

I was already working on becoming a changed woman when I met Lance. I was on this path to figuring out all the things because I had a desire to be a better woman all around. I was tired of my own shit. I assumed I had finally received what I always wanted because I had made that shift in my heart. Now I feel like it was more of a need to heal other parts of me, but first I needed a reason. What greater reason than love? I think it serves as a bonus I caused Lance's divorce, because she could finally find what she truly deserves. She has been a better person Lance and I put together the entire time. She didn't deserve the multiple women before me or me! History will always repeat itself until you change something you do every day.

Lance wasn't even original in his stories, which is very sad. There were so many different women with similar stories. He would take them out (he was so much fun), he would dance, spend money on them, or take them to Codorus for some romance by the water. Sometimes just a dark back road. He would make sure to tell some of them he was a cop and had "people", so they would stay quiet. The problem here is that he was never a cop, but he loved to tell that great tale! I guess intimidation is easier, with a little power. I met other women Lance had been with who had similar tales of heartbreak. I found myself comforting the women who were heartbroken at the hands of my husband. One woman was completely devastated because she was in a month-long relationship with him. He helped her through some tough times during that month, but when she finally gave it up, he created a fight and ghosted her the next day for another woman. She was one of many on a rotating cycle of dating and breaking up. Others were flings from the past he tried to replicate often; some took him up on the offer, others sent me the screenshots. Most were woman who were stuck in a dead-end relationship or were just left devastated from their own partners. He would swoop in to save the day, like he did for me. The knight in shining armor to rescue the broken. My heart broke for them because of his betrayal, I knew exactly how each one of them felt. My heart broke more for the ones that didn't know they would never be the "only one", the ones that were still hooked on him and clung to his every lie. I wasn't surprised at all that there were still more women who thought they were the only one for him. How sad is that? No wonder I tried to deny this reality for so long. Desperately holding it together in hopes I was wrong. I wanted to be crazy, I begged God to just make me crazy. If I had to speak the truth, then I'd have to say I put myself in another domestic abuse situation and stayed longer than I should have, out of shame and embarrassment. Here I was, again allowing someone to treat me this way. I allowed him to cheat on me over and over again even though I truly knew better, simply because I hoped he would get it together like I did. I was no longer an addict and I still allowed him to speak to me with such vile disdain because I wanted the dream he originally promised. It was never real. A person with narcissistic tendencies truly believes they do no wrong. I was never going to win, and my daughters were already choosing the wrong types of guys. I needed to lead by example for them. They needed to know the difference between a good guy and a predator. I needed out.

He became someone I didn't recognize over our time together, I moved out quietly, only providing certain information. At this point he was a loose cannon, so I was not rocking the boat by fighting anything until my children and I were safe. In packing up my bedroom, I found old diaries and gratitude journals with goals and aspirations of being "the best wife ever", determined to figure it out. One of the entries was 18 days before my wedding to Lance. It read, "I'm grateful for my current direction. I know I'm headed the right way even though I'm struggling right now. I'm grateful to have Lance even though he is struggling right now too. We will get through this!" I was desperately trying to make it work alone then. Other things I wrote were mantras I was trying to beat into my own head!

"I will never be asked to forgive more than I have been forgiven."

In one entry I was excited because Lance had finally planned a date and I was excited to see how creative he got! That was followed the next day by mantras such as "I am not angry, I am loved." and the next day's entry "He told me he loved me today!" God my heart breaks for her too. I was so determined then, because one quote said, "You only fail when you quit!" I was trying to program myself to believe I could do it all, while he rested or did whatever he wanted, and I manifested that he did really love me. I constantly talked about needing to find new ways to connect with him intimately, spiritually, and emotionally. He had left me dry, fighting for every drop of love he would toss my way. I held onto this man so hard for so long, because I contributed my sobriety to him. It had nothing to do with the fact I really put in the hard work, effort, and discipline all by myself. Most of the time I had to do it working against him and the added stress he brought to my life. No matter the problem, it was always my fault and his were never addressed. I fell for it all. I desperately searched for peace in yoga, meditation, and church to counterbalance the toxicity at home, still always falling short. I applaud myself for the days I was able to stay calm when he was a wrecking ball, that alone is a superpower.

Angel Number 1111

Your guardian angels are sending you the angel number 1111 to let you know you are experiencing a great spiritual awakening. You are being asked to take control of your own life and strive for independence. Love yourself first and then you will see what you have to share with the world.

But God chose the foolish things of the world to shame the wise; God chose the weak things of the world to shame the strong. God chose the lowly things of this world and the despised things and the things that are not to nullify the things that are, so that no one may boast before him. – **1 Corinthians 1:27-29**

Chapter 11

Healing

It has been said that "The wrong one will find you in peace and leave you in pieces, the right one will find you in pieces and lead you to peace. Lance was definitely all of that and none of that for me at the same time. Whether I found him the correct way or not, whether we had the healthiest relationship or not, we found each other broken and he has guided me to a better version of myself in loving him and dealing with his flaws. I'm naturally a motivated person and wanted to be a better woman all around. I know the process it takes to get great things. I also know the internal struggles and insecurities I fought to be where I am now. I know there will be more I have to go through to get where I'm going. I wish I could say we were creating the foundation for a new us now, leaving space for us to grow or just be. If we can do that right then no matter what, we always know where to go when we need someone to have our back, encourage us to keep pushing forward, or a safe space to be held when we are defeated. That's not the case here. I had to accept defeat and move on.

My first night in my apartment with my babies was the most peaceful night I had in a long time. They had a light in their eyes again. There was laughter and communication between us all. That light had been diminished for so long but I couldn't understand why. I fought so hard to stay with Lance and give them the stability of a two-parent home. Unfortunately, I missed the hurt they saw in me every day because of the treatment I received. They don't need their mom to be married, they need their mom to be happy. My 2022 New Year's Resolution, (the last one I had with Lance and the kids in Tennessee, right before my final flag,) was to end the year toxic-free. It's amazing how fast you can get there when you drop the dead weight.

*****

When I talk about faith, it comes from a place of history. I know what a life of cursing the Lord and never-ending suffering looks like. I lived it. I wake up every day and choose my life of faith because I am so much more authentically me because of his word, his mercy, his love, and his grace. It exists so abundantly in me that I now have enough to share with the world.

Here are some lessons I learned, more than likely the hard way. My hope is someone will skip over some of the unnecessary heartache and B.S. that I caused myself and get to the good stuff quicker!

My Trauma Responses are a learned behavior for lessons I never needed to learn.

I never needed to learn how to protect myself from the abuse of a parent, spouse, or friend, but I did. People go their entire lives and never deal with anything like that. It's not a necessary life skill! It's similar to something my therapist said about addiction- "You are not responsible for why you are an addict; you are only responsible for your sobriety." In other words, you will never be able to get rid of the experience, armor or battle scars you obtained in the middle of your war. You can't always control the situations or events life hands you, but you are responsible for your actions now that the war is over. My problem was realizing I was no longer in that particular war anymore, I was in a smaller battle. I needed to be smarter and choose a different armor for a different battle. I never set the armor down and bandaged my wounds. I just stayed in the battle longer than I should have, not even realizing I was still on guard. I was used to this; I didn't know how to just put everything down and be ok with just being me.

Self-awareness is a blessing and a curse.

Who was I anyway? Who did I want to be? Once I hit my 30's I had some serious soul searching to do. All I know is who I was as a survivor, without ever knowing that I actually WAS a survivor. So basically, I had all the B.S. and all the crazy with no reason for it, and that just creates more guilt and shame. I had made it to the point in my life where I had created those boundaries with my parents, certain siblings, friends, and old ways of life; yet I was still not acting as if I were safe from harm. Making the time to slow down my thought process, recognize my triggers and realize how damaged they all were, was such an eye-opening experience. I started to recognize a lot of my personal relationships in my inner circle were only a slightly better version of my mother, and that was where my serious trust issues came from. It was not until I sat in front of my therapist during our second session, and she told me I have been through some serious trauma and needed help. That is the moment I realized I was the minority here. According to a study published in the journal *Jama Pediatrics*; and based off of confirmed cases reported in the national child abuse database from 2004 to 2011: On Average by the time a child turns 18 years old, 13% have experienced maltreatment (80% involved neglect, 18% were victims of physical abuse, and 9% were victims of sexual abuse.) The risk is higher for younger children under the age of 6, and 81% of these cases were neglected or abused by their parents or immediate caregiver. Up until this moment, I really assumed most people lived some sort of version of what I went through... some better but some worse. And while that still may be true, we are only 13%, I had to admit my life was not the norm here, it was quite the opposite, so more than likely a lot of my behaviors and thought processes were way off too. The amazing part about all of this was I had, over time, already started to do the things

I was supposed to do to heal but didn't know it. I was already doing some things right, and some I needed to tweak. I went strictly no contact with my toxic family members and identified the friends that were just heading in a different direction than where I wanted to go. I remember when I spoke my truth. "I appreciate the time we have had together, the fun times, and the lessons. I am personally just heading in a different direction in my life, and I can no longer tolerate these behaviors in my inner circle. I love you and wish you all the best and hope we cross paths again someday soon." Self-awareness and mindfulness helped me learn to trust my own intuition and take each event as it comes today without yesterday's "hater vision". Don't be afraid to create boundaries, not everyone is meant to be with you the entire journey, and if a boundary makes them leave, that is the best indicator it was necessary.

People who trigger us to feel negative emotions are messengers, showing us the unhealed parts of ourselves.

Our triggers, as the good Pastor said, should be used as sandpaper, polishing the rough and not-so-pretty parts of ourselves until we are left with a smooth and shiny version. I also know that is a hell of a lot easier to say than to actually do! Practice does help, patience, support, and most of all faith. You must get real though and sit with yourself in silence and figure out why he/she gets to you so quickly, or when he/she says that specific phrase, I just lose it. There is a reason and let's face it, you will always be as sick as your secrets. What are you avoiding, or what area of yourself is getting triggered? And if your answer is simply, I don't know, that is a cop-out. You haven't spent enough time with yourself and your own emotions and thought processes. Play detective here and put in the time, effort, and energy into this so you can uncover the "what" and then you can understand the why. I carry a notebook to jot down my feelings and triggers so that I can understand myself better. Part of the reason I wrote this book was to just get it all off my chest. All of the crap that either happened to me, around me, or because of me is now out there. It's no longer a shadow hanging over my life, no one will ever again be able to use it as ammunition against me again. My guilt is finally being released.

As much as I wish I could do some things differently or do over, I can't. All I can say is I'm sorry for my part in mine and other people's personal destruction. I will live every moment as the person I am now, because of it all. I had a lot of anxiety about writing this book, but it was all centered around my own insecurities, someone will definitely hate me now! When you are closer to your assignment, the more your insecurities will surface. Plus, I am a firm believer in sharing your story or testimony, you never know who needs to hear it! I am just finally taking my own advice.

Everybody sucks at something.

Seriously! Even the most talented athletes, actors, musicians, businessmen and women, etc. All suck at something. No one is amazing at all the things and if they are then I bet they are full of insecurities! Either way, you were absolutely given a gift in this life and our purpose in life is to give that gift back to the world. What can you provide to the world to make it a better place? No gift is too big or too small, it is just whether you do it well or not, sometimes it is whether you attempt it at all or not. And sometimes just listening to a friend vent is a gift all on its own. Recognize the moments when you are a part of someone else's blessing. The moments God uses you, pay attention to those. They tend to guide you to your strengths and purpose.

All the faith in the world alone cannot cause the change to occur.

It is similar to the story of the man that was stuck in the middle of the ocean and prayed for God to save him. A man on a boat came by and was ready to help! But the man in the water stated, "No thank you, kind sir, my God will save me!" a little while later a bigger boat came by and again offered assistance, but yet again the man in the water stated, "No thank you, kind sir, my God will save me!" Can you guess what happened next? A third boat came, and they were met with the same response and were turned away. The man eventually drowned and once he reached Heaven, he quickly found God and demanded to know why he had not saved him when he put all his faith in him. The Lord looked down lovingly at his child and said, "Son, I sent you three boats, three opportunities to save yourself, you let them pass by because it was not what you expected." You can have all the favor in the world but if you are waiting for your moment to arrive in a particular package without any effort on your part, you may miss a few other opportunities for things that could turn out better than you have ever imagined. God requires action, he blesses the doers, the givers, and the lovers. The ones that wake up every day and search for ways to be a blessing in other people's lives. The ones that are ready to jump, the moment they see an opportunity. I have found when I search for these "God Moments" I can find other opportunities in different areas of my life that I may not have noticed or been given if I had not participated in someone else's blessing.

Just Cut the Ties now and have Faith it will be replaced with so much more.

God restores all! Let me be clear. This is not me telling you to run the moment something gets rocky. I'm talking about the people that drain you constantly, the abusers, and ego-driven that continue to tear you down, make you feel worthless, and offer no light in your life. The people who are always looking for a fight and it doesn't matter what you do they still complain and bring you down because they are so miserable and don't love themselves. It could also be a dead-end job, that's just as toxic and draining with very few benefits. You know this deep nagging feeling that you have been ignoring. The Universe makes you uncomfortable when change is needed. It is your job to sit with your mess, and really determine if your reactions and responses are causing more of the same, or if this truly is one of those times you must make the break. If it is time to make the break, then chances are it has been a while and you have been fawning your way to this point. When you remove someone whether it is a partner or friend, that leaves a void. It sucks. Plain and simple. How you fill this void will determine if you move forward towards healing or if we are repeating cycles a few more times. Manipulation and control are not love and anyone who uses those tactics to "love" you, is an abuser. Plain and simple. Run.

Fill yourself with the GOOD.

I know I have said this before, but it truly is so important! Seek the Light, in all things. Stay a student and continue your growth. Personal or hobbies! Learn to garden or go to a paint night. For those who know what Board and Brush is, it's so fun and one of my favorite things to do. It doesn't matter the "what" or think about other areas of your life that you could improve on, career advancement, good nutrition, exercise, faith, fun, gratitude, or your relationships. Eat right the majority of the time, exercise most days, go to Church, or seek faith of some kind and have some fun. At the beginning of each chapter is an angel number and a bible verse, all of these have helped me along my journey. Before I focused on my relationship with God in my adult life, I searched for faith in other ways. I would see recurring numbers all the time like 111, 222, 333, etc. I would investigate their meaning and that along with crystals and their healing energies is how I navigated with faith for a while. Once I started truly healing, I realized it was all the same and just another pathway our Gracious Lord has put here for the broken people of the planet to tap into his unconditional love. I have a strong relationship with God now and see a different level of numbers that I have shared with you in this book, but they will always be ever-changing and always evolving if you are too.

We can't forget to add something fun to your calendar at least once a month; whether it is a mini trip, date night, girl's night, book club, or rage room, you pick your poison and make it happen! Put energy into your relationships; this is where the fun on the calendar comes in, or maybe your friend has been struggling so you just show up with dinner or wine and pour it out as they do on the Netflix show, Sweet Magnolia's. Or if your partner has been working hard and long hours so today you decided to do something special. Whatever it is, take time to notice their needs and feelings too, and do your part in nurturing healthy meaningful relationships. Practice gratitude often! I remember looking up at one point in my life and really taking in the full panoramic view of where I'm now, and where I came from. How amazed and proud I felt for actually doing it, even though I was in the midst of another struggle and had no idea how my situation will turn out. I had already done enough; I could die a happy woman who has already achieved so much. It's so important to look back and be grateful for the positive changes and growth you have achieved as well as being grateful for the new obstacles as they are only new opportunities for more positive change and growth.

If you are going to be dumb, you better get tough.

I know it sounds rough, but this one is one of my favorites. I say this to my children often after events like them jumping off the back of the couch trying to be superman, getting hurt then crying! Well, if you would have thought this through before jumping, it may have looked like making sure you had a soft place to land or maybe remembering you can't fly! It's similar if you are doing something you know you are not supposed to be doing, you know you are not, and continue anyway, depending on how bad it is, it could leave you paying for it forever. If you break the law you go to jail; if you lie or cheat in a relationship, you may be left alone to deal with your mess. If you party too much you can fall into that life, and who knows which way that could end. Each choice in life has an equal and opposite reaction. Are you creating a good chain reaction, or not so good? It's a rough time on the not so good side, so if that's the life you choose cool.....just buckle up, it will get tough.

Compete only with yourself.

There is a balance to this because I have and still do seek to learn from others so I can better myself. I didn't have the best role models in my younger years, so I looked at the lives of people on social media. There are so many people some friends and some I have never met in person that I follow because they inspire me. If a feeling of jealousy pops up for something they have done or accomplished, first off, I congratulate them because they actually did it then I ask myself if I would be willing to do what it takes to get there? Like it would be cool to see the summit of Mount Everest, but anyone who really knows me knows I hate the cold and snow, and that Is a lot of training and conditioning to prepare for that type of hike, that frankly, I'm not willing to do what it takes. I would probably be more inclined to put the time in effort into a volcano hike or can we pick a jungle mountain where it is hot? The point is, I am never going to know the entire journey someone took to get to that point but recognizing the things I have done, and accomplished despite my shortcomings is pretty amazing too, considering I would probably be dead by now if I had not seen the light and done something different. There have been times I desperately wanted to know how to do something different, so I reached out to people who have done it and asked them how did you do it? I often asked a bunch of people, because there are so many different ways to get the same end result and I wanted to find one with the tasks I would be willing to do, for example, publishing a book I have written: check! I met with a bunch of different editors and publishers before I decided which route to take, all while knowing one way or another it was going to happen. So, it is totally ok to seek the people that inspire you, just don't let their success keep you frozen because yours may look somewhat different.

What are your three options?

I love options when making a choice. For example, when we bought our camper or any other big purchase item, Lance had a number in mind that we were good with spending. I would ask for three options, one over budget, one under budget, and one on budget. Sometimes I am willing to pay for the upgrades, sometimes I can live with the cheaper model, and sometimes it's right on the money. I do this with almost every decision I make. There are always at least two options if you can't come up with three, maybe not the options you want, but there are definitely choices!

Even my best friend laying in her Hospice bed, losing her battle with cancer had some options. She had a shitty list of options, but they were still there. All you can do in life is play the hell out of the hand you are dealt, options help! If you are trying to decide whether to stay or go, it's not just as simple as staying. You can stay, and continue the way it has been going, which will lead to more of the same. Or you can stay and figure out how to create positive changes in your own life and see how that can have a ripple effect on others. Certain people are never going to be your people no matter how much you want them to be. Some will never change, grow, or evolve to meet you in the direction you want to go. That will never be your responsibility though I'm sure they will make you feel that way. Either way, look at your options and decide for yourself if you were just having a moment and this is truly where you want to be or if it is time for real change and what that change could look like.

Simple does not mean easy.

Pastor Holly Furtick preached this one and I forever follow this advice! God wants you to look for simple, not easy.

Starting a business is not easy, but it can be broken down into a bunch of simple tasks that can be done to start you on the journey. Starting a new workout routine is a simple task, creating a budget is a simple task, quitting smoking is a simple task, or getting your home or office organized is a simple task. None of those are easy! It takes a lot of simple tasks, often with tons of rejection to start a business, A new workout will leave you sore and second-guessing your determination at times, smoking is extremely addictive, and quitting is a rough mental battle for sure, plus for some of us, getting on top of the to-do list is exhausting and never-ending. None of that sounds easy to me but focusing on the simple tasks will help you stay focused when the hard gets in the way and we start talking ourselves out of the things that will get us to our dreams.

Don't listen to the Negative.

There will always be a Debbie Downer that we cross paths with. Whether it is the vile words spewed at you by an abuser, a hurting family member, the Negative Nancy neighbor, the infamous "Karen", or maybe the sound of your own voice on repeat in your head. Just Stop. At the beginning of my healing journey, it was so hard for me to stop the negative voice. My brain was automatically jumping to the conclusions I had heard and learned about myself and life as a child. I was never going to be good enough, people will only love me for what I can do for them, or everybody is lying to me, and I can't trust anyone with my heart fully, they will always end up breaking it anyway. If it's a person for you and you are actively involved in a relationship with a toxic person (friend, family, or partner), that is always degrading, deflecting, gas lighting, or using any other manipulative behavior, please create the boundary. I was told to remind myself if it were God, the Universe, or just great intuition it will be a loving voice, not a scolding one. If all someone spews out is negativity, they don't love themselves, so they will never be able to love you the way you deserve. Well, wouldn't you know once I had put this into practice, it was easy to see the difference. I would have a thought and if it sounded like it was yelling or condescending, I would just say to myself, that is not God's voice, No Thank You, next. In the beginning, I had to sit there for 15 mins sometimes going through thoughts till I found the correct one to plant. Practice makes perfect, and if your thoughts are telling you that you are dumb or stupid or you should have done it this way, it is not coming from love, so discard that B.S. and keep listening. Plus, negativity is a dime a dozen, there are always more than enough people out there complaining about something. Be better.

Most Confidence is Fake.

I learned a long time ago in doing Pure Romance, that almost every woman is just as if not more insecure than you are (men apply too). I guess it's kind of like the picture everyone in their underwear» thing while you are on stage. All I know, is chances are if you see me, I'm insecure. I have an amazing poker face though. I was told to go pretend I had confidence at my next event. Just go pretend, fake it. Simple, not easy. Well, I gave it a try, I had my demo down and practiced what I was going to say, at the party, I pretended I had enough confidence to share with the room, and it was one of the best parties I have ever had. I defiantly did not feel confident at the time, but I acted like it, and looking back now it was easy to do, in the right mindset. I gave those women hope to find their own spark and maybe have a little more fun in life, my passion! Practice makes perfect, and anxiety disappears when you are prepared.

I never realized how much of my past I was carrying in the now. I kept every person I met in my whole life at arm's length because they were just going to leave me anyway if they really knew. I treated myself as the burden I was to my mother. I was socially awkward and assumed everyone really hated me. That is an awesome way to start a new business, right? I had to uncover my true confidence in who I am and who I wanted to be, and the hardest part was being ok with those who wouldn't like me anyway. I had to let go of the subconscious need for love and validation to prove my mother wrong. I really just needed to step into what I already was. I am loved and I have a lot to be confident for. On the opposite end of the spectrum, some people abuse others with their "Confidence" or perhaps a better word here is Ego. Those guys and gals that always seem confident and use that to manipulate others have learned this trick and abuse it. They seek constant validation because they are anything but confident in themselves. They do these things to seek admiration instead of just being helpful or for the greater good. It really is a balance they just can't seem to grasp. Just pay attention to the people who can look you in the eye. That alone says a lot about someone's confidence level. Do you look up and seek connection, or do you always look around and rarely glance up? People give you clues about who they really are and what they really need all the time, your job is to accept what they give you and adjust accordingly.

Create and Love the Life you Live.

I have learned that you don't have to continue down the wrong way just because you have spent so much time there. At any given moment you can set down your baggage, stand up, turn around and walk towards something better. This can be anything from a hobby, a job, a relationship, or personal behavior. You know what is and what is not working for your life, and if you don't, this is the perfect time to spend some time away from the noise and hear your true self. If you want more money, figure out ways you can generate more income, if you want better relationships, figure out better ways to communicate and express yourself, or maybe you just need to slow down and pay attention to those around you and just enjoy their company. Maybe you need to throw away the things and relationships you have outgrown and have the patience that the universe will fill those voids with the correct people when the time is right. Lance and I used to joke about it often because he's "not my type" and I am definitely not his either, we both talk back and challenge each other. This can be good and is actually expected within a healthy relationship. If you are not in a healthy place and willing to learn and grow from your mistakes and those around you, it will never get better. And over time, it will absolutely get worse. What works for one couple doesn't always work for another, it's trial and error but I promise you, very rarely does an abuser wake up and see the error in their ways. The abuse is not worth the good times. Try new things, be open and gracious in the pursuit of happiness. No matter what area of your life could use a little adjustment, you are the conductor! Make a plan and execute the changes necessary to propel yourself to where you want to be. If you don't know where to start, a good place is to have a conversation with someone who did. Manifest your dreams!

God Restores All Things.

Deuteronomy 30:3-4 states: "God, your God, will restore everything you lost; he'll have compassion on you; he'll come back and pick up the pieces where you were scattered. 4 No matter how far away you end up, God, your God, will get you out of there." This is so powerful when you truly believe it. God has restored so much of me and my life already, more times than I can count or deserve. No matter how far you have gone in the wrong direction, you are never too far, and he will meet you where you are, and walk with you back. Put some discipline in your life and just see what opens up. I know that if I have put time, effort, therapy, and all the things to save my marriage just to have to walk away from him anyway, it is because there is a bigger plan for something better. I don't get to always know the destination, sometimes the lord just gives you a direction. Sometimes you just have to get up and start walking, your people will catch up, and the Riffraff will fall off and stay behind. Growth is scary so some people will always be content in their comfortable mess, I refuse that life.

You Cannot Force or Love the addiction out of someone.

It doesn't matter what your addiction is: drugs, alcohol, sex, attention-seeking, shopping, lying, gambling, work, etc. It all causes similar behaviors. Obviously, you add in the extra mind-altering madness with drugs and alcohol, but they are all the same thought processes and basically fill the void we refuse to acknowledge. We just want to be loved, validated, and secure. I got both ends of the spectrum with this! From my personal addiction standpoint, I eventually knew better but didn't want better enough. No one's ultimatums, threats, or well wishes would have saved me until I was ready to admit I needed to be saved and willing to put in the work to fix it myself. On the flip side, most addicts will deflect with anger on the subject. We push our loved ones and those closest to us away because ultimately, we are ashamed. It's a vicious cycle and unfortunately, the only way to break it is not to participate. In my healing journey at first, I was completely transparent with all aspects of my life. I wanted everyone to know I was now a trustworthy person. Now I realize I actually shouldn't be so transparent with everyone. I give too much access to a lot of the wrong people, and predators look for that. I have always been guarded, but I was guarding the wrong parts of me and giving away so freely the ones I should have been guarding better. This is why they say you attract what you are. I was a broken toxic mess. You absolutely learn to love yourself first, then it is so much easier to recognize the people of the world who also love themselves, that's where you start looking for your tribe. I am a way better judge of character because I have a better character now. You attract what you are, so become what you need first, the rest will always work itself out.

Abuse is abuse, no matter what their "Title" is.

I just love people who demand respect because they are your mother, father, husband, wife, maybe it's a mother-in-law or father-in-law. How about the bossy aunt or uncle? Maybe yours is the narcissistic sibling or friend? Some of us are lucky to meet these people as our bosses or coworkers. Either way, I come from a place where my own mother has let me down more times than I can count, so your behavior must match the type of respect you want, in order to receive it from me. Actions speak louder than words, and I match toxic energy with grace and distance. Just telling me to respect you, when you haven't done anything to deserve it, doesn't work for me anymore. I need a little less talk......you know the rest!

Do better when you learn better.

I still followed in my momma's footsteps more times than I'd like to admit. I thought my love for Lance was better and truer because it avoided the physical violence between each other. He never hit me. A happy and healthy relationship avoids all the things that could hurt your partner or hinder the relationship. I hadn't recognized those red flags, in fact, I had ignored them completely. I held on so long because I did what I wanted and got all the tangible things I wanted. Lance willingly gave me things that were important to me because they kept me off his back. I got the amazing wedding, a 3-carat diamond ring, all the trips, bougee gifts, and all the things money could buy. At first, I thought he really cared because why else would be doing all these things for me? Then I realized we were not going anywhere real. Lance wouldn't work on a budget with me either. I knew there was a lot of money missing but I couldn't prove where it had gone. When I would question it, he would just make it harder for me to figure out where it went. I reflect on a time a former inmate reached out and asked if I really knew the type of man that I had married. Or a customer he did a new roof for but never delivered on the bonuses he promised. His word never meant anything. He was a fraud. We weren't closer in connection or intimacy in fact we were further apart. He looked for every excuse and validating reason for his horrible behavior at home and his love of other women. It was all ok because I was crazy. I decided I was just going to be crazy somewhere else. It's not always easy to make the big moves or do the uncomfortable things, but staying miserable to avoid the scary, keeps you from the incredible.

Do it Scared.

I can't think of anything I wasn't scared to do at first. Now there are different levels of fear, whether it's starting a new workout class and not knowing anyone, going skydiving for the first time, or maybe it's a public speech. Even to the opposite end of the spectrum like leaving your abuser to live alone in a safe environment, or actually being honest and telling someone about the dysfunction around you. Regardless of what level of fear we are talking about, if you feel it, the right path is close. You take that class, write that song, publish that book, go on that trip, leave that so wrong for you douche canoe that does nothing but hold you back, he (she) is ugly anyway! If you fail, do it again, I recommend making some adjustments first. Learn, grow, attempt, repeat. Do it scared, every time, it gets a little easier, and you learn to be a little braver. You will never be quite ready, but the Universe will always listen to the Brave.

Angel Number 1211

Angel Number 1211 is saying to pay attention to your reoccurring thoughts about yourself and your life. It's a message from your angels not to be hindered by old habits that need to be changed. Look to new opportunities with Optimism as they will bring out favorable effects and positive outcomes.

All this is for your benefit, so that the grace that is reaching more and more people may cause thanksgiving to overflow to the glory of God.

2 Corinthians 4:15

Chapter 12

With Gratitude

There are so many people I need to thank for having such a huge impact on my life. First, I want to thank God. For his never-ending love and grace. There have been so many desperate situations in my life where he was the only one that showed up, and there were tons of those moments he showed up and I didn't even know it was him at. He certainly didn't get the glory he deserved for keeping me alive more times than I can count. You find ways to lead me even when I'm stubborn and try to do it on my own. Thank you.

To my 4 Amazing children: Brooklyn, Lexi, Trenton, and Phoenix. Thank you for being uniquely you, for teaching me how to be a better mom every day, and for loving me more on the days I fail. I hope you always carry these lessons in this book that have helped me and know that you never have to carry someone else's baggage to feel whole. Continue to do the big, scary, and risky things! You will always have a better story of almost making it, than of those who never tried. I am so proud of each of you for your own individual growth and accomplishments so far, I believe in you all and will always be your biggest fan.

To the amazing women in my life, I looked up to as amazing mothers or Inspirations; All of My Grandmothers, My Aunt Vicky, Lisa, Margie (Mom), Leann Rhodes and so many more I know from work, social media, or met in passing along the way. I am forever grateful for the impact you have made on my life and my family's life. The love and support my children and I have received from you all have helped shape the woman I am now, Thank you so much.

To Rob and Pam, I just love you both. Thank you for teaching me about Real Estate, life, and so much more. I'm so grateful to have you both in my life and through my struggles, you guys have been such a blessing. I will never know how I got so lucky to meet you, Thank you.

To My Beautiful Barbie, Goodness what a dull world this is going to be now. You lit a big part of my life for a long time. There was not one thing you didn't know about me, and you loved me and showed up anyway. Every single time, no matter what. You have been the only one. Such a Beautiful, amazing soul that I am so lucky to have called my Friend. I am truly sorry you were not able to fulfill your promise (to literally half the world) for your glorious "I Am Better Party" you really did deserve it and I am going to miss the shit out of you. You are my Person Babe! Barbara Ann Jones April 21,1977-March 26, 2022 #F**kCancer

To My fellow Pure Romance Sisters, share your stories and keep spreading the word. Women need to hear your story to fight for their own, and the service we provide is so needed. Keep empowering women in all areas of their lives to grow and radiate self-love. Thank you for always filling my cup with your positive vibes and motivation. Pure Romance Consultants are some of the most amazing, goal-oriented, loving women ever. Thank you.

To Lance, I am so grateful to have learned so many lessons because of you. I am the woman I am today because of life with you. Thank You and Many Blessings to you.

And finally, to everyone else that I have met along the way. If we crossed paths before and I was a nightmare, I am so sorry and thank you for dealing with that person, she didn't know any better at the time and was extremely broken. I wish I could right all my wrongs from the past and do things differently. All I can say is you should meet me now, let's start over. If you are someone I had to walk away from, thank you for the love and lessons from the past, and many blessings to you for your future. To everyone who is trying to heal from things they don't talk about, thank you for being here and making me a part of your journey. I am always available if you need a listening ear, please reach out. No one knows you're internally suffering if you keep it a secret. Keep seeking the light, it is always worth it!

And to those that made it, and broke the cycle for themselves and their children, Thank you! You have created one less, and I'm so proud of you!

I will NEVER forget where I came from because I will do whatever it takes to never go back to who I was and what I tolerated before. I owe myself the biggest apology for putting up with what I didn't deserve. I thank the Lord above every day for showing me the light, if he can bring me out of such darkness and can restore my heart and soul after everything I have been through and caused, he can certainly do that for you. Who am I to receive such favor? From a nobody girl who grew up on the wrong side of the tracks and learned how to survive in chaos, transformed into a woman that has such love for herself and the people she meets, who is finding her voice to stand up for what's right in the face of bully's and those who choose to win by intimidating. He has restored me into a healed and happy woman in love with her babies, career, and self. He will do the same and more for you if you are ready and willing to do the work to become a more Radiant version of YOU.

When the time is right, I, the Lord will make it happen – **Isaiah 60:22.**

Many blessings to you and yours always.

Final Thoughts

People with narcissistic tendencies will always blame someone else for the issue at hand, it will always be your fault, no matter if it really is or not. Their goal is to create confusion, so you think it is your fault and there is always reasonable doubt. That is where they love to keep you. I kept the secret of what life was really like living with my mother, previous abusers, and Lance. In this relationship, I hid the fact he would always criticize what I didn't do, never accounting for the million other things I did that day. It was always about my shortcomings. It put me in a place where I was so ashamed, that I didn't even tell my best friend half of it. I was doing 90% of everything around the house and with the kids, animals, and chores, and I was making most of the money that he took and spent on his women or gambled it away. He shut me up and kept me happy with gifts and trips or half-ass sex. He had brought zero value to my life for a long time, and I was refusing to accept it because of what I'd seen him do at the beginning (Love Bombing). I knew who he could be and what he promised me in the beginning. If I loved a little harder or was a little more compassionate, he would come back to me. I also saw who he was for the multiple ladies he met and the B.S. stories he told them.

His favorite excuse was going to check on a job or pick up materials. That was his out to visit them. He left his crew and job sites for the same reasons. I had put so much time and effort into trying to figure out how to bring back the man of my dreams, and he was just trying to find ways to control me better. When I left, he tried to threaten me, when I didn't respond, he had his friends try. He hacked into my messages and showed up on dates I had planned with friends. He took everything from me when I left, and I didn't fight for any of it, I just let the things and the people that were attached to him go. His attempts to intimidate me probably would have worked if I didn't have so much love and support around me during this time.

I forgive myself for believing his lies. I am no longer ashamed that I was at one point so hopelessly in love with this man because of the dream he promised. I'm no longer afraid to admit he hurt me more times than I can count, and it took me a while, but I finally see the light. I forgive myself for wanting love so bad I settled and tried to force it into existence. I forgive myself for being wrong about him but now I'm so grateful because I walked away healed. I deserved better and I was going to create it elsewhere and share my story in hopes of helping someone find the strength to say no more for themselves.

When an abuser is losing control, they grasp at straws. I was no longer afraid of his crazy behavior, or reactions, I just wanted it to end. That's where they hope to keep you. Exhausted and no longer willing to fight. Keep stepping forward!

There are monsters in every corner of this world, that's not who you are supposed to stop and try and fix. Love them and pray for them from afar, protect yourself and your space for the people that will love you always and not just what you can do for them. If this sounds like home, stand up, be smart, get help, and make a plan. You are worthy of basic human needs, love, and support. If you need out there are so many ways, reach out to someone you trust, a shelter, the police, or me, let's make a plan to get you to safety. You deserve the peace that you keep desperately trying to create at home. You are not alone, safety in numbers. You got this!

"You own everything that happened to you. Tell your stories. If people wanted you to write warmly about them, they should have behaved better." – Leann Rhodes

National Domestic Abuse Hotline:

1(800)-799-7233

Text START to 88788

Thehotline.org

National Suicide Prevention Lifeline

1(800)-273-8255

Suicidepreventionlifeline.org

National Alliance on Mental Illness Helpline

1(800)-950-6264

Nami.org

National Drug Helpline

1(844)-289-0879

Crisis Text Line

Text HOME to 741741

References

Pastor Steven and Holly Furtik, Elevation Church. https://elevationchurch.org

Specific Sermons: Say Yes To Simple | Holly Furtick | Elevation Church,

https://youtu.be/g5G0JzsCkHM

When Never Meets Now | Pastor Steven Furtick | Elevation Church, https://youtu.be/2N8yPkL3Isk

Jamilia White, https://inspiredjamila.com, Trauma Response post, https://m.facebook.com/249222445101726/photos/a.2492 35148433789/3631944533496150/?type=3&source=57

Fight, Flight, Freeze, Fawn: Examining The 4 Trauma Responses, https://www.mindbodygreen.com/articles/fight-flight-freeze-fawn-trauma-responses

Odds Of Abuse And Mistreatment Add Up Over Children's Lives, https://www.npr.org/sections/health-shots/2014/06/02/318227196/odds-of-abuse-and-mistreatment-add-up-over-childrens-lives

Cindy Cherie. www.cindycherie.com

Made in the USA
Middletown, DE
30 April 2023

29508898R00109